THE TEN FOOT SQUARE HUT

AND

TALES OF THE HEIKE

The Hō-ō or Cloistered Emperor Go-Shirakawa

THE
TEN FOOT SQUARE HUT
AND
TALES OF THE HEIKE

Being two thirteenth-century
Japanese classics, the "Hōjōki"
and selections from the
"Heike Monogatari"

translated by
A. L. SADLER, M.A.

CHARLES E. TUTTLE COMPANY
Rutland, Vermont & Tokyo, Japan

Representatives
Continental Europe: BOXERBOOKS, INC., *Zurich*
British Isles: PRENTICE-HALL INTERNATIONAL, INC., *London*
Australasia: BOOK WISE (AUSTRALIA) PTY. LTD.
104-108 Sussex Street, Sydney 2000

Published by the Charles E. Tuttle Company, Inc.
of Rutland, Vermont & Tokyo, Japan
with editorial offices at
Suido 1-chome, 2-6, Bunkyo-ku, Tokyo, Japan

© *1972 by Charles E. Tuttle Co., Inc.*

Library of Congress Catalog Card No. 72-157261

International Standard Book No. 0-8048-0879-1

First edition published 1928 by Angus & Robertson Ltd., Sydney
First Tuttle edition published 1972
Seventh printing, 1983

PRINTED IN JAPAN

The illustrations are taken from the edition of Genroku II. (1699) with the exception of the frontispiece which is from a reproduction of an original in possession of the Imperial University of Tokyo, and that of the Shirabyōshi, which is from the work entitled "Hissei Musha Suzuri," by Ooka Shunboku 1736.

THE COURT AND GOVERNMENT

The Emperor (Tenno)

The Cloistered Emperor   The Retired Emperor
(Hō-ō)   (In or Shin-in)

Sessho ... ... Regent
Kwampaku ... Chief Minister

THE DAJO-KWAN (SUPREME COUNCIL)

Dajo-daijin ... Prime Minister

Minister of the Right   Naidaijin   Minister of the Left
Udaijin   Minister of Interior   Sadaijin

Dainagon ⎫
Chūnagon ⎬ Councillors
Sangi   ⎭

Udaiben	Secretaries			Secretaries	Sadaiben
Uchuben	of the	**Shonagon**		of the	Sachuben
Ushoben	Right			Left	Sashoben

OFFICIALS OF THE EIGHT DEPARTMENTS

Hyobu	War	Nakatsukasa	Intermediary
Gyobu	Justice	Shikibu	Ceremonies
Okura	Treasury	Jibu	Civil
Kunai	Imperial Household	Mimbu	Home

In each department were
Kyo   Taiyu   Suke   Jo

MILITARY OFFICIALS

Konoe-fu ... The Imperial Bodyguard

(Udaisho)		(Sadaisho)	
Ukon-e-no-Taisho	Generals	Sakon-e-no-Taisho	Generals
Chūjō	of the	Chūjō	of the
Shosho	Right	Shosho	Left

Emon ... The Imperial Gateguard

Uemon-no-Taisho	Saemon-no-Taisho
Chūjō	Chūjō
Shosho	Shosho

Below whom were Emon or Efu-no-Kami

Taiyu
Suke
Jo

Uma-ryo ... Horseguard

Uma-no-Kami	Right Master	Sama-no-kami	Left Master
Suke	of the Horse	Suke	of the horse
Jo		Jo	

ECCLESIASTICAL TITLES

Dai-Sōjō Archbishop ⎫
Sōjō Bishop   ⎬ Ranks
Sōzu   ⎪
Risshi   ⎭

Zasshu Lord Abbot

Ajari (Sk. Ajariya)   Instructor of Disciples

Hōin ⎫
Hōgen ⎪
Hōkkyo   ⎬ Titles of Honour
Kwasho (Tendai) ⎪
Washo (Hosso) ⎪
Oshō (other sects) ⎭

Hōshi	Priest
Biku (S. Bikshu)	Monk
Bikuni (S. Bikshuni)	Nun
Ubasoku (S. Upasaka)	Lay Believer
Ubai (S. Upasika)	Female Lay Believer

ILLUSTRATIONS

INTRODUCTION

THE translations here presented comprise the Hōjōki or Ten Foot Square Hut, and selections from the Heike Monogatari or Story of the Heike Clan, both of them masterpieces of Japanese literature of the thirteenth century, and dealing with the same period from a different point of view. The Hōjōki consists of the reflections of a recluse who had retired in disgust from a world that was too full of violent contrasts and cataclysms, both of animate and inanimate nature, to allow a sensitive person to find it at all tolerable. If, though there are some Japanese scholars who question it, tradition ascribes this work truly to Kamo-no-Chōmei, it was disappointment at not being allowed to succeed to the ancestral position of Lord Warden of the Shrine of Kamo in Kyoto that caused him to forsake the world and go to live in the hills.

As can be seen from the Heike Monogatari, which describes the period in more detail, Chōmei was not singular in being thus arbitrarily deprived of position and income, neither was he the only one who sought refuge in nature and Buddhist philosophy. At least two of the highest in the land did so too, for we read in the Heike Monogatari that "Seirai and Shinhan, thinking it was no use remaining at Court in such an age, even if they became Counsellors of State, retired from the world while still young, Mimbu-kyo Nyūdō Shinhan having the hoar-frosts of Ohara for company and Saisho Nyūdō Seirai living among the mists of Kōya, both had no thought for anything but attaining enlightenment in the next existence." And then there is the sad case of the Dowager Empress Kenrei-mon-in, the description of whose cell on Ohara is so like that of Chōmei as to suggest that it may have been the original, supposing the Hōjōki to be a compilation of a slightly later date. Be that as it may none of these distinguished recluses have left to posterity so charming a picture of their retirement as has the author of the Ten Foot Square Hut. Content with his simple but tasteful and natural existence, "a friend of the moon and the wind," he spends his days with literature and music, varied by rambles over the hills, contemplating the ever-changing landscape, and visits to places of historic associations, especially those connected with hermits like himself. He lived in the twelfth century, but six hundred years had passed since the introduction of Buddhism and all the culture that accompanied it, and long before that the Japanese were a civilized and tasteful people, and the literary output of all these centuries in prose and verse had not been small, so that the language of the Hōjōki and the Heike Monogatari is a well developed and pliant medium, concise and elegant and expressive. And because these classical works have always been regarded as models of prose, there is not so much difference between the writing

of that day and the present, far less than there is
between the English of Chaucer who wrote a century
later and modern English. This is one advantage of
the use of an ideographic script perhaps, for though
sounds change ideographs do not.

The taste for a retired life of elegance has always
been and still is characteristic of the Japanese temperament, as is evident from the popularity of the
philosophy of Cha-no-yu or Teaism, which enables
even busy people to become temporary hermits in the
Tea-room, to be in the world though for a while
not of it, like the "moon in the market-place." The
fixing of the size of the Tea-room as four and a half
mats, the size of Chōmei's hut, indicates its descent
from the cell of the Buddhist recluse Vimalakirrti who
miraculously entertained in it the Buddha and three
thousand five hundred of his saints and disciples, and
has as it were crystallized and handed down the mood
of Chōmei as a historico-philosophical "retreat" for all
who wish to refresh their souls by temporary retirement.

Chōmei was, like most of the aristocrats of his race,
an agnostic, though he found the art and ritual of
Mahayana Buddhism as it was practised in Japan quite
diverting. Thought has ever been free in his country,
for Buddhism is a philosophy and Shinto simply an
expression of the national temperament, though we find
that the feeling of the pathos of things inspired by
the Way of Gautama certainly had a softening influence on the rather ruthless spirit of the military
men.

It is the narrative of the Heike Monogatari that supplies the background of Chōmei's meditations and tells the story of what was the most dramatic rise and fall of any ruling family in the history of the Empire. After the long peace of the Nara and Heian periods from the seventh till the twelfth centuries, during which the Court Nobles of the house of Fujiwara administered the country under the Mikado, and art and literature and Buddhist ritual flourished in and around the Imperial capitals of Nara and Kyoto, suddenly a quarrel broke out between rival factions at Court, and the military clans of Gen and Hei, or Minamoto and Taira as they may also be called, who had so far acted as frontier forces against the barbarian Emishi and Imperial Guards and Police of Capital, were drawn in on opposite sides, with the result that after the battle they claimed the spoil and were no longer content to be underlings to the Courtiers.

And since the dominion of the whole country was a prize worth holding they were not so content to divide it as they had been their constabulary duties, but fought another war to decide who should prevail. From this emerged Taira Kiyomori as military dictator of the Empire in 1159. Then began a glorious though brief period of prosperity for his family and supporters, including even a few of the Minamoto who had thrown in their lot with him, like that esthetic old warrior Minamoto Yorimasa, famed for his poems and his archery, when not to be a Taira was not to be a man. His sons and his grandsons and nephews filled all the high offices of Minister and Commander of the Imperial Guard, while his sister-in-law was married to the Hō-ō or Cloistered Emperor Go-Shirakawa and his daughter to his son the Emperor Takakura. Kiyomori was probably one of the greatest of the brilliant group of autocrats who have administered Japan from that time to this, but unfortunately for his family he allowed himself to be persuaded to spare the lives of the children who were heirs to the headship of the rival clan, Yoritomo and Yoshitsune. This error of judgment was not lost on Yoritomo who made no such mistake. And so through these two, though not till after his death, downfall came swiftly on his house.

For the elegance of the Imperial Capital has never been favourable to the military spirit, and the men of the eastern provinces and central hills had kept their hardiness better than the younger generation of the Heike. And this also Yoritomo perceived, and made his own military capital in the east accordingly, and there it has mostly remained till the present day. And Kyoto is a quiet retreat for those whose business is philosophy or etiquette or the arts and crafts. It lies in a hollow surrounded by hills, a situation that was not ideal for defence when these hills were tenanted by monasteries full of soldier-priests, nor was it conducive to a bracing climate, though eminently picturesque.

But even before the death of the redoubtable Lay-priest Chancellor of the Heike there were two abortive revolts instigated by dissatisfied Courtiers who had felt the length of his arm, and connived at by the Cloistered Emperor, Go-Shirakawa. The first of these is notable for the pathetic story of the exile of several of these

Nobles and the second for the gallant fight at the Uji
River and the deaths of Minamoto Yorimasa and
Prince Mochihito, son of Go-Shirakawa who was
involved with him. Here the turbulent warrior-priests
of the great monasteries of Hieizan, Miidera and Nara
showed the most unclerical side of their nature and
fought for place and power as they never fought for
doctrine. These monasteries were a constant menace
to the Capital and to all who differed from them on
these secular questions, and even the Sovereign hardly
cared to oppose them, though since most of the younger
Imperial children became Prince-Abbots, his interests
and theirs were usually identical.

It was the military leaders the clerics disapproved of
most, for these feared neither God nor Devil nor
Buddha. And when later on the Minamoto rose under
Yoritomo and got the Cloistered Emperor to issue an
Edict against the Heike, it was the eccentric priest
Mongaku who acted as a go-between for the military
chief, though he had incurred the wrath of the Sovereign by jumping over the Palace wall and interrupting
a musical performance to ask the Court for a subscription to his temple. And it was the temporary alliance between Kiso Yoshinaka, one of the Minamoto leaders,
with the priests of Hieizan that enabled him to seize
the Capital and drive the Heike out.

The Heike then fled with the young Emperor Antoku
and his mother, Kiyomori's daughter, and the Nii-no-
Ama or Nun of the Second Court Rank, Kiyomori's
widow, and the Three Sacred Treasures that are the
Imperial Regalia, in ships down the Inland Sea, and

after attempting to establish themselves in Kyushu, returned and fixed their temporary capital at Yashima in the island of Shikoku. Meanwhile internal strife had broken out among the Minamoto between Kiso Yoshinaka, the "Rising Sun General," and Yoritomo, head of the clan. Yoritomo was a cold calculating autocrat, and his wife was another, according to some authorities rather more so, and of a type that might be called Turkic, so deadly was he to members of his own family. Probably he was jealous of Yoshinaka's prowess, as he was later on of that of his brother Yoshitsune. And since Yoshinaka was no Courtier and his men were among the roughest in the land he soon came first to words and then to blows with the Court as well as with the priests and people of the Capital. This resulted in his being so discourteous as to burn the Palace and cause the death of more than one high ecclesiastic, so that the Hō-ō in indignation asked Yoritomo to chastise him.

This he was most willing to do, and sent his brothers Yoshitsune and Noriyori against him with a large army, and he was defeated and slain with his four "Demon Kings" Imai, Higuchi, Tate and Nenoi, after a very gallant fight from which only the lady warrior his consort Tomoe escaped alive. She was one of the many ladies of strong mind depicted in this work, which incidentally demonstrates, if that is necessary, that the Japanese lady has other qualities than the deferential elegance usually attributed to her.

Meanwhile the Heike had come back to the mainland and entrenched themselves at Ichi-no-tani, not far from the modern city of Kobe, and Yoshitsune moved on to turn them out of this strong position between the hills and the sea.

After a great battle he succeeded, chiefly by his daring and famous ride down the cliffs of Hiyodori to take them in the rear. As they fled to their ships many of their leaders were killed or captured in the fight on the shore and the rest got away again to Yashima. Here Taira Tadanori, the Mirror of Chivalry, was killed and the young Atsumori, and here Shigehira was taken alive. But Yoshitsune quickly followed up his success by dashing across the straits in a violent storm, when he was hardly expected, and burning them out of their stronghold. At this battle of Yashima several famous combats took place, in which the Heike leaders Tomomori, Kagekiyo, and the mighty archer Noritsune distinguished themselves by their gallantry and Munemori, the head of the clan, by his vacillating pusillanimity. The Heike were unfortunate in their chief, for had their forces been led by Tomomori or Noritsune, it is possible that the final tragedy might have been averted.

As it was, however, there was nothing for them but to wander aimlessly down the Inland Sea, and here, in the straits of Akamagaseki near the modern Moji, they were brought to bay and the last great battle was fought in which, partly owing to treachery, they were utterly defeated and the leaders and the Nii-no-Ama the wife of Kiyomori with the child-Emperor in her arms, scorning to surrender, sprang into the sea and perished in the waves. Such is the outline of their tragic story, and little remains to add except that after the extermination of those of Taira blood who still survived, the cold and implacable Yoritomo was able to seize the administration and persuade the Emperor to appoint him Shogun or Military Dictator, an office which his family managed to hold with little interruption right up to the Restoration of 1868. And so deep an impression did the gallant deeds and pathetic incidents of these few years make on the feelings of the men of letters of the time that two distinct works came to be composed, one, the shorter recension, a series of recitations for the Biwa player, which forms the Heike Monogatari, and a longer and more detailed historical account known as the Gempei Seisuiki or Rise and Fall of the Minamoto and Taira.

Thus the Heike Monogatari corresponds somewhat to the Song of Roland or the Sagas of Europe, with which it is more or less contemporary. And owing to the genius of the Japanese people for retaining what is best and most inspiring in their ancient customs, the art of the Biwa player is still a living one, and his recitations of the deeds of these ancient heroes now mingle with the equally stirring ones of the centuries that have followed, up to the Russo-Japanese war and even the Great War. And nothing affects a Japanese audience more than these martial ballads. At any particularly tense passage this feeling shows itself in a spontaneous exclamatory shout from some of the listeners which recalls the "Aoi" of the old French Ballad; supposing that explanation of this expression to be correct.

But the Heike Monogatari differs from the Song of Roland in being more historical and also in being written in poetical prose and not in verse. Both works are alike, however, in most probably having been composed by priests who had forsaken fashionable society owing to disappointment, Thorold, at irritation from not receiving preferment and the Lay-priest Yukinaga* at a lapse of memory in the course of a discussion on music. And it is interesting to note that Andrew Lang observes that for some reason or other the greatest war poems in Europe have been inspired by glorious defeats, such as those of Maldon, Flodden, Roncesvaux, and Culloden. And to these we may add the prose poem of the Heike Monogatari in Japan.

---

*cf. the statement of Yoshida Kenko (1281-1350) in the Tsuregure-gusa.

In the time of the Retired Emperor Go-Toba (1184-1221) Yukinaga former Governor of Shinanao was renowned for his knowledge of musical matters, so that he was once summoned to take part in a discussion about them, but forgetting two of the "Dances of Seven Virtues," he was given the nickname of "The Young Master of Five Virtues," and this he took so much to heart that he forsook his studies and became a recluse. But the priest Jichin, who would take in anyone, however low his rank, if he had any artistic gift, felt sympathy for him and provided him with what he needed. It was this lay-priest Yukinaga who wrote the Heike Monogatari and taught a certain blind man named Jobutsu to recite it. He wrote specially well about the affairs of the temples of Hieizan, and his detailed knowledge of Yoshitsune enabled him to describe him graphically. Of Noriyori he does not seem to have had so much information, for he omits much concerning him. For what pertains to the warriors and their horses and arms, Jobutsu, who was a native of the East Country, was able to tell him what he had learned from these warriors themselves. And the Biwa players of the present day imitate the voice of this Jobutsu.

And it is not only in the Biwa recitations that these stories are preserved, but in the Nō dramas, very many of which are drawn from this work, as well as in the popular theatre and Jōruri or popular ballads and the narratives of the professional storytellers.

Buddhist sentiments play the same part in these narratives as the Christian religion does in the medieval literature of Europe, but, since they are philosophical, do not produce the fanatic frame of mind that derives from religion. This is seen very well in the story that describes Kiyomori, disliked as he was by the priests for his violence to them, as a reincarnation of a Buddhist Saint, and his evil deeds as indispensable in the scheme of things as were those of Devadatta in the life of Buddha. With such an impartial eye does the Buddhist philosopher regard the drama of life that in this narrative it is not very easy to see with which side his sympathies really lie. This is rather a notable trait in the people of his race, who usually seem able to regard such things rather impersonally and enjoy the emotional feeling of a tragedy for the thing in itself.

The priest-soldiers of the great monasteries of Hie-izan, Miidera, and Nara, who are so often represented as stirring up trouble in the Empire, and who are specially referred to by the Emperor as one of the things over which he had no control, were no more credit to Buddhism than were the monks of many medieval establishments to Christianity, and their habits were just about as contrary to the precepts of their founder as were those of the latter. But monasteries everywhere tended to become dens of thieves, and it may be said that the quarrels of these warlike monks were entirely about material matters, and they rarely, if ever, indulged in sectarian persecution.

The verses that occur in these texts have been put into the same form as the Japanese metre of five, seven, five, seven, seven syllables. Unfortunately it is impossible to represent in any other language the allusive word-play that is a feature of Japanese verse, so much of the meaning must necessarily be lost.

The selections from the Heike Monogatari are taken from my translation of the whole in the Transactions of the Asiatic Society of Japan, Vols. XLVI and XLIX, somewhat revised. A new version has been made of the Hōjōki, since the excellent translation of F. V. Dickins has been long out of print.

A.L.S.

THE HŌJŌKI

CEASELESSLY the river flows, and yet the water is never the same, while in the still pools the shifting foam gathers and is gone, never staying for a moment. Even so is man and his habitation.

In the stately ways of our shining Capital the dwellings of high and low raise their roofs in rivalry as in the beginning, but few indeed there are that have stood for many generations. This year falling into decay and the next built up again, how often does the mansion of one age turn into the cottages of the next. And so, too, are they who live in them. The streets of the city are thronged as of old, but of the many people we meet there how very few are those that we knew in our youth. Dead in the morning and born at night, so man goes on for ever, un-enduring as the foam on the water.

And this man that is born and dies, who knows whence he came and whither he goes? And who knows also why with so much labour he builds his house, or how such things can give him pleasure? Like the dew on the morning glory are man and his house, who knows which will survive the other? The dew may fall and the flower remain, but only to wither in the morning sun, or the dew may stay on the withered flower, but it will not see another evening.

During the forty years or so that I have lived since I began to understand the meaning of things I have seen not a few strange happenings.

In the third year of the era Angen,* and the twenty-eighth day of the fourth month I think it was, the wind blew a gale, and at the hour of the Dog (8 p.m.) a fire started in the south-east of the Capital and was blown across to the north-west. And everything as far as the Shujaku Gate, the Daikyoku Hall and the Office of Internal Affairs was reduced to ashes in a single night. They say it started at Higuchi Tominokōji in a temporary structure used as a hospital. Now as the flames came on they spread out like an opened fan, and the remoter houses were smothered in smoke while those nearer roared up in flames. The sky was dark with ashes and against this black background the fire glowed red like early dawn, while everywhere the flames driven by the wind went leaping on over a space more than a hundred yards wide. And of those caught by it some fell choked in the smoke, while others were overtaken by the flames and perished suddenly. And those few who managed with difficulty to escape were quite unable to take their goods with them, and how many precious treasures were thus lost none can tell.

Of the Palaces of the Great Nobles sixteen were entirely destroyed, and of the houses of lesser people

*1175 A.D.

the number is unknown. One-third of the city was burnt and many thousands must have perished, and cattle and horses beyond reckoning. The handiwork of man is a vain thing enough in any place, but to spend money and time on building houses in such a dangerous spot as the Capital is foolish indeed beyond measure.

Then again in the fourth year of the era Jisho, the fourth month and about the twenty-ninth day a great typhoon blew with immense violence from the neighbourhood of Naka-no-Mikado and Kyōgoku toward Rokujō. For the space of near a quarter of a mile it raged, and of the houses within its reach there were none, great or small, that it did not throw down. Of some the whole house fell flat, and of others the roof of the gate was taken off and blown it may be some five hundred yards. Others again had their boundary walls levelled, so that there was nothing between them and their neighbour's premises. Household treasures were blown up into the air and destroyed and pieces of board and shingles filled the air like driven leaves in winter. The dust was as thick as smoke, and the roar of the wind so loud that none could hear the other speak. I suppose the bitter wind of Karma that blows us to Hell could not be more savage or fearsome.

And not only were the houses damaged, but a number of people were lamed and hurt in trying to repair them. This whirlwind eventually veered round to the south-west and fresh shouts of distress arose. It is true these winds are not infrequent, but yet there were very many who said: "Ah, this must be the portent of some dreadful happening."

And in the Waterless Month (sixth) of the same year suddenly and without warning the Capital was changed. And this was a most extraordinary thing, for they say that the Capital was first fixed here in the August Age of the Mikado Saga, and so it has remained for all these centuries. And thus to change it without any good reason was a very great mistake, and it was no wonder that the people should complain and lament. Still that was, of course, quite unavailing, and all the inhabitants, beginning with His August Majesty the Mikado, and the Ministers and Great Nobles of the Court, had perforce to remove to the new Capital at Naniwa in Settsu.

And of those who wished to get on in the world who would stay in the former Capital? All who coveted Court Rank, or were the expectant clients of some great lord, bustled about to get away as soon as possible. It was only a few unadaptable people who had nothing to hope for, who stayed behind in the ancient Capital.

And those mansions that stood so proudly side by side from day to day became more ruinous. Many were broken up and floated down the river Yodo, while their pleasure grounds were turned into rice-fields. And the fashions changed also in these days, so that every one came to ride on horseback, while the more dignified ox-car was quite forsaken. And everybody was scrambling to get land by the Western Sea and none cared for manors in the north and east.

Now it happened at this time that I chanced to go down myself to the new Capital in the province of Settsu. And when I came to look at it the site was cramped and too narrow to lay out the Avenues properly. And the mountains towered over it to the north while the sea hemmed it in on the south and the noise of the waves and the scent of the brine were indeed too much to be borne.

The Palace was right up against the hills, a "Log-hut Palace" built of round timbers. It all seemed so very strange and rough, and yet somehow not a little elegant. And as for all those houses that had been broken up and brought down, so that the river was almost dammed up by them, I wondered wherever they were going to put them, for still there was so much empty ground, and very few dwellings had been built. So the old Capital was already a waste and the new one not yet made. Every one felt as unsettled as drifting clouds. And the natives of the place were full of complaints over losing their land, while the new inhabitants grumbled at the difficulty of building on such a site. And of the people one met in the streets those who ought to have been riding in carriages were on horseback and those who usually wore court costume were in military surcoats. The whole atmosphere of the Capital was altered and they looked like a lot of country samurai. And those who said that these changes were a portent of some civil disturbance seemed to be not without reason, for as time went on things became more and more unquiet and there was a feeling of unrest everywhere.

But the murmurings of the people proved of some effect, for in the following winter they were ordered back to the Ancient Capital. But all the same the houses that had been destroyed and removed could not at once be restored to their former condition.

Now we learn that in the dim ages of the past, in the August Era of a certain most revered Mikado, the Empire was ruled with great kindness: that the Palace was thatched with reeds and its eaves were not repaired, because it was seen that little smoke went up from the houses, and the taxes were on that account remitted. So did the sovereign have pity on his people and help them in their distress. When we compare it with these ancient days we can well understand what a time we live in. And if this were not enough, in the era Yōwa* I think it was, but so many years have elapsed that I am not certain, there were two years of famine, and a terrible time indeed it was. The spring and summer were scorching hot, and autumn and winter brought typhoons and floods, and as one bad season followed another the Five Cereals could not ripen. In vain was the spring ploughing, and the summer sowing was but labour lost. Neither did you hear the joyous clamour of the harvest and storing in autumn and winter.

Some deserted their land and went to other provinces, and others left their houses and dwelt in the hills. Then all sorts of prayers were said and special services recited, but things grew no better. And since for

_____

*1181 A.D.

everything the people of the Capital had to depend on the country around it, when no farmers came in with food how could they continue their usual existence? Though householders brought out their goods into the street and besought people to buy like beggars with no sense of shame, yet no one would even look at them, and if there should be any ready to barter they held money cheap enough, but could hardly be brought to part with grain. Beggars filled the streets and their clamour was deafening to the ears.

So the first year passed and it was difficult enough to live, but when we looked for some improvement during the next it was even worse, for a pestilence followed, and the prayers of the people were of no effect. As the days passed they felt like fish when the water dries up, and respectable citizens who ordinarily wore hats and shoes now went barefooted begging from house to house. And while you looked in wonder at such a sight they would suddenly fall down and die in the road. And by the walls and in the highways you could see everywhere the bodies of those who had died of starvation. And as there was none to take them away, a terrible stench filled the streets, and people went by with their eyes averted. The ordinary roads were bad enough, but in the slums by the River-bed there was not even room for carts and horses to pass.

As for the poor labourers and woodcutters and such like, when they could cut no more firewood and there was none to help them, they broke up their own cottages and took the pieces into the city to sell. And what one man could carry was hardly enough to provide him with food for one day.

And it was a shocking thing to see among these scraps of firewood fragments with red lacquer and gold and silver foil still sticking to them. And this because those who could get nothing else broke into the mountain temples and stole the images and utensils and broke them up to sell for kindling. It must be a wretched and degenerate age when such things are done.

Another very sad thing was that those who had children who were very dear to them almost invariably died before them, because they denied themselves to give their sons and daughters what they needed. And so these children would always survive their parents. And there were babies who continued to feed at their mother's breast, not knowing she was already dead.

Now there was a noble recluse of the Jison-in Hall of the Ninnaji temple called Ryūgyō Hō-in and entitled Lord of the Treasury, who out of pity for the endless number of dead arranged for some monks to go round the city and write the syllable "A" on the foreheads of all they found, that they might receive enlightenment and enter Amida's Paradise. And the number that they counted within the city, in the space of four or five months, between the First and Ninth Avenues on the north and south and between Kyōgoku and Shujaku on the east and west, was at least forty-two thousand three hundred. And when there is added to this those who perished before and after this period, and also those in the River-bed and Shirakawa and

Western City quarters, they must have been almost beyond count. And then there were all the other provinces of the Empire. It is said that not long ago in the August Age of the Mikado Sutoku-in in the era Chōshō* there was such a visitation. But of that I know nothing. What I have seen with my own eyes was strange and terrible enough.

Then in the second year of the era Gen-ryaku† there was a great earthquake. And this was no ordinary one. The hills crumbled down and filled the rivers, and the sea surged up and overwhelmed the land. The earth split asunder and water gushed out. The rocks broke off and rolled down into the valleys, while boats at sea staggered in the swell and horses on land could find no sure foothold. What wonder that in the Capital, of all the temples, monasteries, pagodas and mausoleums, there should not be one that remained undamaged. Some crumbled to pieces and some were thrown down, while the dust rose in clouds like smoke around them, and the sound of the falling buildings was like thunder. Those who were in them were crushed at once, while those who ran out did so to find the ground yawning before them. If one has no wings he cannot fly, and unless one is a Dragon he will find it difficult to ride the clouds. For one terror following on another there is nothing equal to an earthquake.

Among those who suffered was the child of a warrior some six or seven years old. He had made a little hut under the eaves of the earthern wall and

---

*1132 A.D.   †1184 A.D.

was playing there when the whole fell and buried him. And it was very sad to see how his parents cried aloud in their grief as they picked him up all battered and with his eyes protruding from his head. Even a stern samurai at such a time thought it no shame to show signs of his deep feeling. And indeed I think it quite natural.

The worst shocks soon ceased, but the after tremors continued for some time. Every day there were some twenty or thirty that were beyond the ordinary. After the tenth and twentieth day they gradually came at longer intervals, four or five, and then two or three in a day. Then there would be a day and then several without any shock at all, but still these after shocks lasted, it may be three months.

Of the four elements, water, fire, and wind are always doing damage, but with the earth this is comparatively rare. It was in the era Saiko.* I think, that there was a great earthquake, and the head of the Great Buddha in the Tōdaiji at Nara fell, which I consider a very sad loss indeed, but it is said to have been not so severe as the one I have described.

On these occasions it is the way of people to be convinced of the impermanence of all earthly things, and to talk of the evil of attachment to them, and of the impurity of their hearts, but when the months go by and then the years, we do not find them making mention of such views any more.

Thus it seems to me that all the difficulties of life

---

*540 A.D.

spring from this fleeting evanescent nature of man and his habitation. And in other ways too the opportunities he has of being troubled and annoyed by things connected with his locality and rank are almost infinite.

Suppose he is a person of little account and lives near the mansion of a great man. He may have occasion to rejoice very heartily over something, but he cannot do so openly, and in the same way, if he be in trouble it is quite unthinkable that he should lift up his voice and weep. He must be very circumspect in his deportment and bear himself in a suitably humble manner, and his feelings are like those of a sparrow near a hawk's nest. And if a poor man lives near a wealthy one he is continually ashamed of his ill appearance and has to come and go always with an apologetic air. And when he sees the envious glances of his wife and the servants, and hears the slighting way in which his neighbour refers to him, he is always liable to feel irritable and ill at ease. And if a man has little land round his house he is likely to suffer in a conflagration, while if he lives in an out of the way place it is awkward for travelling and he is very liable to be robbed.

Men of influence are usually greedy of place and power, while those of none are apt to be despised. If you have a lot of property you have many cares, while if you are poor there is always plenty to worry you. If you have servants, you are in their power, and if you compassionate others then that feeling masters you. If you follow the fashions around

you, you will have little comfort, and if you do not
you will be called crazy. Wherever you go and whatever you do it is hard to find rest for mind and body.

I inherited the estate of my great-grandmother on
the father's side, and there I lived for a while. But
then I left home and came down in the world and
as there were very many reasons why I wished to
live unnoticed, I could not remain where I was, so
I built a cottage just suited to my wants. It was
only a tenth of the size of my former home and con-
tained only a living-room for myself, for I could not
build a proper house. It had rough plastered walls
and no gate, and the pillars were of bamboo, so it
was really nothing more than a cart-shed. And as
it was not far from the River-bed there was some
peril from floods as well as anxiety about thieves.

So I went on living in this unsympathetic world
amid many difficulties for thirty years, and the various
rebuffs that I met left me with a poor opinion of this
fleeting life. So when I arrived at the age of fifty
I abandoned the world and retired, and since I had
no wife or child it was by no means difficult to leave
it, neither had I any rank or revenue to be a tie to hold
me. And so it is that I have come to spend I know
not how many useless years hidden in the mists of
Mount Ohara. I am now sixty years old, and this
hut in which I shall spend the last remaining years
of my dew-like existence is like the shelter that some
hunter might build for a night's lodging in the hills,
or like the cocoon some old silkworm might spin. If
I compare it to the cottage of my middle years it is

not a hundredth of the size. Thus as old age draws on my hut has grown smaller and smaller. It is a cottage of quite a peculiar kind, for it is only ten feet square and less than seven feet high, and as I did not decide to fix it in any definite place I did not choose the site by divination as usual. The walls are of rough plastered earth and the roof is of thatch. All the joints are hinged with metal so that if the situation no longer pleases me I can easily take it down and transport it elsewhere. And this can be done with very little labour, for the whole will only fill two cart-loads, and beyond the small wage of the carters nothing else is needed.

Now hidden deep in the fastnesses of Mount Hino, I have put up eaves projecting on the south side to keep off the sun and a small bamboo veranda beneath them. On the west is the shelf for the offerings of water and flowers to Buddha, and in the middle, against the western wall is a picture of Amida Buddha so arranged that the setting sun shines from between his brows as though he were emitting his ray of light, while on the doors of his shrine are painted pictures of Fugen and Fudō.* Over the sliding doors on the north side is a little shelf on which stand three or four black leather cases containing some volumes of Japanese poems and music and a book of selections from the Buddhist Sutras. Beside these stand a harp and a lute of the kind called folding harp and jointed lute. On the eastern side is a bundle of fern fronds and a mat of straw on which I sleep at night. In the

---

*The Bodhisattvas Samanta Bhadra and Akshobya.

eastern wall there is a window before which stands
my writing-table.   A fire-box beside my pillow in
which I can make a fire of broken brushwood com-
pletes the furniture.   To the north of my little hut I
have made a tiny garden surrounded by a thin low
brushwood fence so that I can grow various kinds of
medicinal herbs.   Such is the style of my unsubstantial
cottage.

As to my surroundings, on the south there is a
little basin that I have made of piled-up rocks to
receive the water that runs down from a bamboo spout
above it, and as the forest trees reach close up to the
eaves it is easy enough to get fuel.

The place is called Toyama.   It is almost hidden in
a tangled growth of evergreens.   But though the valley
is much overgrown it is open toward the west, so that
I can contemplate the scenery and meditate on the enlightenment that comes from the Paradise in that
quarter.   In the spring I behold the clusters of
wistaria shining like the purple clouds on which Amida
Buddha comes to welcome his elect.   In the summer
I hear the cuckoo and his note reminds me that he will
soon guide me over the Hills of Death of which they
call him the Warden.   In autumn I hear everywhere
the shrilling of the Evening Cicada and inquire of
him if he is bewailing the vanity of this fleeting life,
empty as his own dried up husk, while in winter the
snow as it piles up and melts seems like an allegory
of our evil Karma.

If I get tired of repeating the Invocation to Buddha
or feel disinclined to read the Sutras, and go to sleep

or sit idly, there is none to rebuke me, no companion to make me feel ashamed. I may not have made any special vow of silence, but as I am all alone I am little likely to offend with the tongue, and even without intending to keep the Buddhist Commandments, separated from society it is not easy to break them.

In the morning, as I look out at the boats on the Uji River by Ōkanoya I may steal a phrase from the monk Mansei and compare this fleeting life to the white foam in their wake, and association may lead me to try a few verses myself in his style. Or in the evening, as I listen to the rustling of the maples in the wind the opening lines of the "Lute Maiden" by the great Chinese poet Po-chu-i naturally occur to my mind, and my hand strays to the instrument and I play perhaps a piece or two in the style of Minamoto Tsunenobu. And if I am in the mood for music I may play the piece called "Autumn Wind" to the accompaniment of the creaking of the pine-trees outside, or that entitled "Flowing Waters" in harmony with the purling of the stream. I have little skill in verse or music, but then I only play and compose for my own amusement, and not for the ears of other people.

At the foot of the hill there is a little cottage of brushwood where lives the keeper of these hills. And he has a boy who sometimes comes to bear me company, and when time is heavy on my hands we go for a walk. He is sixteen and I am sixty and though the difference in age is so great, we find plenty of amusement in each other's society.

Sometimes we gather the Lalong grass or the rock-pear or help ourselves to wild potatoes or parsley, or we may go as far as the rice-fields at the foot of our hills and glean a few ears to make on offering to the deities. If the day is fine we may climb up some high peak and look out over the Capital in the distance and enjoy the views of Mt Kobata, Fushimi, Toba or Hatsukashi. Fine scenery has no landlord, so there is nothing to hinder our pleasure.

When I feel in the mood for a longer walk we may go over the hills by Sumiyama past Kasatori and visit the temple of Kwannon of the Thousand Arms at Iwama. Or it may take our fancy to go and worship at the famous temple of Ishiyama by Lake Biwa. Or again, if we go by Awazu, we may stop to say a prayer for the soul of Semi Maru* at his shrine on Ausaka Hill, and from thence may cross the River Tagami and visit the grave of Saru Maru Taiyu.†

Then on our way back, according to the season, there will be the cherry-blossoms to pluck and the maple or the bracken or some sort of berries to gather. And of these some we can offer to the Buddha and some we can eat ourselves.

In the quiet evenings I look out of my window at the moon and think over the friends of other days, and the mournful cry of the monkey often makes me moisten my sleeve with tears. I might imagine the cloud of fire-flies to be the fishing-fires at Makinoshima, or the rain at dawn to be the patter of the leaves driven

---

*Famous lute-player, 10th Century. †Poet of the same period.

by the wind. When I hear the hollow cry of the pheasant that might be mistaken for a father or mother hallooing to their children, as Gyogi Bosatsu's verse has it, or see the mountain deer approach me without any fear, then I understand how remote I am from the world. And I stir up the embers of my smouldering fire, the best friend an old man can find by him when he wakes. The mountains themselves are not at all awesome, though indeed the hooting of the owls is sometimes melancholy enough, but of the beauties of the ever-changing scenery of the hills one never becomes weary. And to one who thinks deeply and has a good store of knowledge such pleasure is indeed inexhaustible.

When I first came to live in this place I thought it would be but for a little space, but five years have already passed. This temporary hut of mine looks old and weatherbeaten and on the roof the rotting leaves lie deep, while the moss has grown thick on the plastered wall. By occasional tidings that reach me from the Capital, I learn that the number of distinguished people who have passed away is not small, and as to those of no consequence it must be very great indeed. And in the various fires I wonder how many houses have been burnt.

But in this little impermanent hut of mine all is calm and there is nothing to fear. It may be small, but there is room to sleep at night, and to sit down in the day-time, so that for one person there is no inconvenience. The hermit-crab chooses a small shell and that is because he well knows the needs of his own body. The fishing-eagle chooses a rough beach because he does not want man's competition. Just so am I. If one knows himself and knows what the world is he will merely wish for quiet and be pleased when he has nothing to grieve about, wanting nothing and caring for nobody.

It is the way of people when they build houses not to build them for themselves, but for their wives and family and relations, and to entertain their friends, or it may be their patrons or teachers, or to accommodate their valuables or horses or oxen.

But I have built mine for my own needs and not for other people. And for the good reason that I have neither companion nor dependant, so that if I built it larger who would there be to occupy it? And as to friends they respect wealth and prefer those who are hospitable to them, but think little of those who are kindly and honest. The best friends one can have are flowers and moon, strings and pipe. And servants respect those who reward them, and value people for what they get. If you are merely kind and considerate and do not trouble them they will not appreciate it. So the best servant you can have is your own body, and if there is anything to be done, do it yourself. It may be a little troublesome perhaps, but it is much easier than depending on others and looking to them to do it.

If you have to go anywhere go on your own feet. It may be trying, but not so much so as the bother of horses and carriages. Every one with a body has two servants, his hands and feet, and they will serve his will exactly. And since the mind knows the fatigue of the body it works it when it is vigorous and allows it to rest when it is tired. The mind uses the body, but not to excess, and when the body tires it is not vexed. And to go on foot and do one's own work is the best road to strength and health. For to cause trouble and worry to our fellows is to lay up evil Karma. And why should you use the labour of others?

Clothes and food are just the same. Garments woven from wistaria-vines, and bed-clothes of hemp, covering the body with what comes nearest to hand, and sustaining one's life with the berries and fruits that grow on the hills and plains, that is best. If you do not go into society you need not be ashamed of your appearance, and if your food is scanty it will have the better relish. I do not say these things from envy of rich people, but only from comparison of my early days with the life I live now.

Since I forsook the world and broke off all its ties, I have felt neither fear nor resentment. I commit my life to fate without special wish to live or desire to die. Like a drifting cloud I rely on none and have no attachments. My only luxury is a sound sleep and all I look forward to is the beauty of the changing seasons.

Now the Three Phenomenal Worlds, the World of Desire, the World of Form, and the World of No-form, are entirely of the mind. If the mind is not at rest, horses and oxen and the Seven Precious Things and Palaces and Pavilions are of no use. With this lonely cottage of mine, this hut of one room, I am quite content. If I go out to the Capital I may feel shame at looking like a mendicant priest, but when I come back home here I feel compassion for those who are still bound by the attraction of earthly things. If any doubt me let them consider the fish. They do not get tired of the water; but if you are not a fish you cannot understand their feelings.* Birds too love the woods, but unless you are yourself a bird you cannot know how they feel. It is just so with the life of a hermit: How can you understand unless you experience it?

Now the moon of my life has reached its last phase and my remaining years draw near to their close. When I soon approach the Three Ways of the Here-after what shall I have to regret? The Law of Buddha teaches that we should shun all clinging to the world of phenomena, so that the affection I have for this thatched hut is in some sort a sin, and my attachment to this solitary life may be a hindrance to enlighten-ment. Thus I have been babbling, it may be, of use-less pleasures, and spending my precious hours in vain.

In the still hours of the dawn I think of these things, and to myself I put these questions: "Thus to forsake the world and dwell in the woods, has it been to dis-cipline my mind and practise the Law of Buddha or not? Have I put on the form of a recluse while yet my heart has remained impure? Is my dwelling but a poor imitation of that of the Saint Vimalakirrti while my merit is not even equal to that of Suddhipanthaka the most stupid of the followers of Buddha? Is this poverty of mine but the retribution for the offences of a past existence, and do the desires of an impure

*Looks like an echo of the well-known passage in Chuang-tz.

heart still arise to hinder my enlightenment? And in my heart there is no answer. The most I can do is to murmur two or three times a perchance unavailing invocation to Buddha."

The last day of the third month of the second year of the era Kenryaku. By me the Sramana Ren-in in my hut on Toyama Hill.

> Sad am I at heart
> When the moon's bright silver orb
> Sinks behind the hill.
> But how blest 't will be to see
> Amida's perpetual light.

---

*1212 A.D.

THE HEIKE MONOGATARI

The sound of the bell of Jetavana* echoes the impermanence of all things. The hue of the flowers of the teak-tree declares that they who flourish must be brought low. Yea, the proud ones are but for a moment, like an evening dream in springtime. The mighty are destroyed at the last, they are but as the dust before the wind.

If thou ask concerning the rulers of other countries far off; Chao Kao of Ch'in, Wang Mang of Han, Chu I of Liang, Lu Shan of T'ang, all these, not following in the paths of the government of all the Kings and Emperors who went before them, sought pleasure only; not heeding remonstrance nor considering the disorders of their country, having no knowledge of the affliction of their people, they did not endure, but perished utterly. So also if thou inquire concerning our own country, Masakado in the period Shohei, Sumitomo in Tenkyo, Gishin in Kowa, Shinrai in Heiji, all were arrogant and bold of heart in divers manners, yet if we consider what is told of the former Prime Minister Prince Taira-no-Ason Kiyomori, the Lay-priest of Rokuhara, of a more recent time, neither in their words nor their intentions were they his equal.

---

*The monastery park of Buddha at Sâvatthi.

The Lay-Priest Chancellor Taira Kiyomori.

Now the reason for this great prosperity of the Heike was said to be the favour of Kumano Gongen. And this was the manner of it; when Kiyomori was yet only styled Aki-no-kami, he went to worship at Kumano by ship from Anonotsu in Ise, and a large "Suzuki" fish sprang up into his vessel, as it is related in former times that a white fish leaped into the ship of Wu Wang of Chow, and however it may have been he attributed it to the favour of the Gongen. As we have said, he was on religious pilgrimage, so that he was observing the ten prohibitions, abstaining from animal food and making purifications, yet departing from these, he cooked the fish himself and ate of it and gave also to his retainers who were with him. And afterwards nought but good fortune attended him and he at last became Prime Minister. His posterity too attained high office more quickly than a dragon ascends the clouds, greatly excelling in happiness the nine generations of their ancestors.

Boy Attendants

Now Prince Kiyomori, being overtaken by illness on the eleventh day of the eleventh month of the era Ninan, at the age of fifty-one, retired from the world and took monk's vows to save his life, assuming the religious name of Jōkai. As the result of this, his sickness departed and he was cured, fulfilling the decree of destiny. Yet after his retirement from the world he did not put an end to his luxurious living. People obeyed him as grass before the wind, and depended on him as the earth does on the rain that moistens it. If one speaks of the Princes of the house of Rokuhara, they were most noble and illustrious, and none might be considered equal to them. Moreover as for the brother of this Lay-priest's wife, Taira Dainagon Tokitada—all those who did not belong to his house were to be considered people of no position, so that every one was wishing to make alliance with him. From the manner of wearing the Eboshi* to the style of the crest on clothes, everything must be in the fashion of Rokuhara; so that every one from one end of the land to the other studied it.

Now however wisely a king or ruler may govern, or in the case of the political actions of Regent or Prime Minister, it is a usual thing that certain worthless fellows will gather together to speak ill of him; but against this Lay-priest in his prosperity there was not even a casual breath of reviling. And for what reason? Even because, by the device of this Monk-regent, about three hundred youths of from fourteen to sixteen years old, with their hair cut short and wearing red robes, were everywhere patrolling the streets of the Capital. And if there was anyone who spoke evil against the Taira, and one of these chanced to hear it, straightway summoning to him his fellows, they would violently enter that man's house, seize his treasures and household goods and bring him bound to Rokuhara. So that none were found to open their mouth about the things they saw or knew. At the very name of the

---

*Black cap of ceremony.

Kamuro of Rokuhara every one, both pedestrians and those who rode in carriages, made wide room and passed by on the other side. Even when entering or leaving the forbidden gate of the Palace, it was not necessary to declare their name, for the officials of the city looked with averted eyes where they were concerned.

THE SPLENDOUR OF KIYOMORI

Not only did Kiyomori himself live in splendour and luxury, but all his house likewise shared his prosperity. His eldest son Shigemori was Naidaijin and Sadaisho, his second son Munemori was Chūnagon and Udaisho, his third son Tomomori was Chūjō of the third grade, his eldest grandson Koremori Shosho of the fourth grade; sixteen of his house in all held offices of the higher grade while thirty had right of entry to Court. The whole number of his family who drew revenues from the provinces as military officials was about sixty persons. All others appeared as of no account in the world.

Now Nippon Akitsushima has but sixty-six provinces, and of these the domains of the Heike were thirty; almost half the land. Beside these the manors, rice-fields and gardens that they possessed were without number. In the multiplicity of their gorgeous costumes they were resplendent as the flowers of the field; the noble and illustrious crowded before their gates like a throng in the market-place: the gold of Yang Chow, the jewels of King Chow, the damask of

A Shirabyōshi.

Wu, the brocade of Shuh—of the seven rarities and the myriad treasures not one was lacking. For poetry and music, fishing and riding, perchance even the Mikado's Palaces were not more renowned.

Giō

Now not only did this priestly statesman hold the whole country in the hollow of his hand, but, neither ashamed at the censure of the world, nor regarding the derision of the people, he indulged in the most surprising conduct. For example, in the Capital there were two famous Shirabyōshi* who were sisters, named Giō and Ginyō, both young girls and very skilled in their art. The elder, Giō, was beloved by Kiyomori, and her younger sister also was in high favour with every one. So they were enabled to build a good house for their mother, who was granted a monthly income of a hundred koku of rice, and a hundred kwan in money by Kiyomori. Their family was consequently rich and honoured, fortunate beyond the lot of most people. Now the origin of Shirabyōshi in our country was in the reign of Toba-in when Shima-no-senzai and Wakano-mae appeared as dancers. In the beginning the Shirabyōshi wore the Suikan or silk court robe and Tate-eboshi or black court headdress, with a white dirk in their belt, when they danced, and it was like the dancing of a man: but from the middle age the headdress and sword were disused, and they danced only

*Shirabyōshi "White Rhythm Makers." Dancers, the prototype of the modern Geisha.

in the white Suikan, hence they were called Shira-byōshi.

But among the Shirabyōshi of the Capital, when they heard of the good fortune of Giō, there were some who hated her and some who were envious. Those who envied her said: "Ah! how fortunate is Giō Gozen, if we do even as she does we too may become prosperous in like manner;" so they added the syllable "Gi" to their names to see if they too might not obtain good luck. Some called themselves Giichi, Giji, Gifuku, or Gitoku. Those who hated her said, "Surely it is not a matter of the name or character with which it is written, fortune is the result of disposition inherited from a previous existence;" and so few of them took such a name.

Now it came to pass that, three years afterwards, another skilful Shirabyōshi appeared; and she was a maiden sixteen years of age, born in the province of Kaga, and her name was Hotoke. And when the people of the Capital, both high and low, saw her, they said that although from of old times many Shira-byōshi had been seen there, one so dexterous as she had not been beheld; and she too was in exceeding great favour with all. And in the course of time Hotoke Gozen said: "Though I have made sport for the whole Empire, yet this great Taira minister who now is the source of all fortune and prosperity has not yet deigned to summon me; after the manner of entertainers I will e'en go uninvited." So she forthwith proceeded to the Palace in Nishi-hachijo. On her arrival, a servant entered the presence of the minister and announced:

"Hotoke Gozen, now so famous in this city is without." Then the Lay-priest grew very angry and replied "How then! do not these players attend only when they are called? Why it is that she has come unbidden? Whether she be called God or Buddha, (Hotoke) it is not suitable that she come here while Giō is present. Bid her depart at once."

Hotoke Gozen was already retiring at these unkind words, when Giō said to the Minister "It is surely the usual custom that players should attend unbidden, and moreover it is because she is still young and innocent that she has thus intruded on you—so it will be most unkind to speak harshly and send her away—how greatly will she be shamed and distressed by it; as I myself have trodden the same path, I cannot but remember these things. If you will not deign to allow her to dance or to sing, yield, I pray you, so far as to call her back and receive her in audience; if you then dismiss her, it will be a favour indeed worthy of her deep gratitude." To this the Priest-Minister answered: "Since you wish it to be so, I will see her and then dismiss her:" and he sent a servant to call her.

Hotoke Gozen, having been thus harshly treated, was even then entering her carriage to return when she was summoned and turned back again. The Minister met her and granted her an audience. Thus Hotoke, though it seemed unlikely that she would gain an audience, yet through the kindness of Giō, who thus importuned for her, was not only able to enter the Minister's presence, but further it happened that he,

wishing to hear her voice, directed that she should sing
a song of the kind called "Imayo:" and thus she sang:

When I first enjoyed the sight of your bountiful presence,
'Twas like the evergreen pine, flourishing age after age.
Like to the pond on whose rocks is basking the turtle
    thrice blessed,
Numberless storks beside it happily preening their wings.

And those who heard it were greatly wondering at
her skill and her beauty, and pressed her to repeat it
even to three times. The Lay-priest also was greatly
diverted and said: "Since you are so skilful at Imayo
you must also be able to dance well; we wish to see
one of your dances." Then the drums were ordered
to be beaten and she danced forthwith. Now Hotoke
Gozen was renowned for the beauty of her hair and
features, and her voice was no less exquisite; how
then should she fail in the dance?

So when she put forth all her skill and charm in
dancing, Kiyomori was enraptured and his heart
turned wholly toward her. But when Hotoke Gozen
said to him: "Did I not present myself uninvited, and
when almost rejected was I not only brought back by
the entreaty of Giō Gozen? I pray thee grant me leave
that I may return quickly;" the Lay-monk by no
means agreed to the proposal, and thinking that she
was only embarrassed because of the presence of the
other, proposed to send Giō away.

But Hotoke Gozen answered "How can this be? If
we were to remain here both together, I should be
most embarrassed, and if your Excellency send away
Giō Gozen and keep me here alone, how ashamed will

she not feel in her heart? Indeed it will be most painful to her. If you deign to think of me again in the future, I am always able to come at your call. I beg that to-day I may be allowed to retire."

Kiyomori, seeing how the matter lay, straightway ordered Giō to leave the Palace, and to that end sent a messenger three times. Although Giō had expected this thing from long before, she did not think that it would come to pass to-day or to-morrow. But as the Nyūdō continually repeated this unreasonable demand, there was nothing for her but to sweep her room clean and to go. Even those who meet under the shade of the same tree, or who greet each other by the riverside, since it is owing to relations in a previous existence, ever feel pain at parting with each other; how much more grievous a thing it is, when two have been together in affection for the space of three years. So in regret and grief she shed unavailing tears. Thus as it was a thing that must be, Giō went forth, but ere she went she wrote on the shōji this verse, thinking to bring perchance to remembrance the forgotten image of one who was gone.

> Whether fresh and green
> Or in sere and yellow leaf,
> Grasses of the field,
> When the autumn comes at length,
> Meet with the same hapless fate.

Then riding in a carriage to the place where she lived, she cast herself down within the shōji and wept unceasingly. Her mother and her younger sister, seeing these things, asked many questions, but Giō would by no means give any answer, and only by inquiring of her maid did they come to know what had happened. Moreover the hundred koku and hundred kwan of monthly allowance ceased; it was now the turn of the relations of Hotoke Gozen to taste the enjoyment of this prosperity. Soon all the people of the Capital heard of these matters, and wondered if it were true that Giō had been dismissed from the Nishi-hachijo Palace. There were some who went to see her, some who sent letters, and some who sent their servants, but Giō, since she had no inclination to amuse anyone now, did not even receive their letters, neither did she treat in any way with the messengers. She became more and more melancholy and only shed unavailing tears. Thus the year ended and the next spring came.

Then Kiyomori sent a messenger to Giō asking after her affairs and her health and saying that as Hotoke Gozen wished for some one to beguile her tedious hours, would she not come up to the palace to dance, or it might be sing Imayo, and thus cheer her, but Giō returned no answer, only she lay down and restrained her tears. Again he sent to know why she did not go, or why at least she did not answer. When her mother heard this, weeping bitterly, she thus admonished her: "Why at least do you not deign to send an answer? and why do you not go when thus rebuked?" At which Giō said, restraining her tears: "If I thought I ought to go, I would answer, but since I shall by no means go, I know not what answer I can give. As I do not go when I am thus summoned, he has somewhat to discuss with me, he says; and what may this be but per-chance to drive me from the city, or it may be to take my life. Beyond these two things no worse is possible. Even though one go forth from Miyako, the way is not so sorrowful. Again if one is called away from life, would one grudge this body so much? Once having known the bitterness of being disliked, shall I look on his face a second time?"

Now when she did not feel it necessary to reply, her mother again admonished her, weeping: "Among those who dwell in this land, the commands of Taira Min-ister ought not to be disobeyed, and moreover the relation of man and woman is from a former exist-ence, it does not begin in this life; even though the pledge be for a thousand or ten thousand years, there are many who soon are parted, and though some think that it will be but for a little while, yet it may endure unto the end of life. The thing that has no certainty in this life of ours is the relation between man and woman. If you do not go now when you are sum-moned, it is not likely that you will be put to death, but certainly we shall be driven from Miyako. Even if you must leave the Capital, you are both still young, and can make shift to find shelter somewhere or other; but I am old, and when weak and declining, to go and live in a strange place, is sad even to think of. Oh that I might be allowed to live and die in Miyako!"

Thus considering her filial duty both in this life and the next, though Giō had determined that she would not go, not disobedient to her mother she stood ready to set out, bathed in tears; indeed her feelings were very pitiable. As it would be lonely for her to go alone, her younger sister, Ginyō prepared to accompany her, with two other Shirabyōshi beside, making in all a company of four. In one carriage they rode together and came to the Nishi-hachijo Palace.

On entering however, she was not called to take the seat she had formerly occupied, a place much lower down being provided for her. "Alas!" thought she, "how shall this be? Although there is no fault in me, and although I have come hither, how am I distressed in being given a lower seat." And not knowing what to do, she said nothing to anyone, but her tears fell plentifully from beneath the sleeve she pressed to her face. When Hotoke Gozen saw this, she was greatly affected and said to Kiyomori: "It would have been better if you had not sent for her; but now let her be called up hither, or if not, suffer me to be dismissed and go away."

The Lay-priest would not at all consider this and would not permit her to go away, but by and by he deigned to receive Giō and to greet her and inquire how she did, explaining that, as Hotoke Gozen was lonely, it would be very pleasant if Giō would comfort her by dancing and singing Imayo. "Indeed I came wishing not to disobey your august command," replied Giō and sang the following verse of Imayo:—

Even Buddha himself was once an ordinary person,
I also at last like unto Buddha shall grow.
Everything on this earth can partake of the nature of
    Buddha.
Only to be prevented, that would be painful indeed.

Twice she sang it, weeping bitterly, and as she sang all the Princes and Courtiers of the Heike and the high officers and samurai shed tears of admiration and sympathy. Kiyomori also acknowledged the justice of her complaint and frankly confessed it before them all.

So when the dance was finished he intimated that, as at present he had to attend to other matters, in future she should come without any especial summons to dance and sing and amuse Hotoke. But Giō, repressing her tears, went forth without returning any answer.

Thus Giō, not having intended to go, but thinking it cruel to disobey her mother, a second time suffered ignominious treatment. How pitiable it was indeed! Then thinking that if she remained in this world, she was always liable to meet with such afflictions, she determined to put an end to her life. Her sister Ginyō, hearing this, also made up her mind to die with her.

Then their mother, being aware of their resolve, again with tears more gravely admonished them. "If you have determined to do this, how greatly do I regret that I persuaded you to go; for in truth your chagrin is the cause of this, and if you take your life and your sister follow you, what profit is it to me your mother, who am aged and declining, if I still live on? I also will die with you. Now to cause one's mother, who has not yet attained the limit of her years, to cast her life

away, is it not even as one of the five great sins?* This
life is but a temporary abiding place, shame upon
shame even, what is it to be accounted? There is only
sadness of heart in the long darkness of this world. If
in this life we become attached to things, in the next
life we must tread an evil way in sadness." Thus
melted in tears she persuaded them.

Giō, also weeping, admitted that she spoke truth;
doubtless it was as one of the five great sins that, because of regret at being put to shame, she should
determine to put an end to her life. So it was that
she gave up her intention of dying by her own hand:
but since if she should stay in Miyako she would still
be liable to humiliation, Giō, at the age of only one and
twenty, deserted the Capital and became a nun. In a
mountain village in the recesses of Saga, building herself a hut of brushwood, she continually murmured
her invocations to Buddha. When her sister Ginyō
perceived that she did thus, having made compact to die
with her, how much more when the world has become
so hateful shall she not at least accompany her sister.
So at the age of nineteen she changed her condition,
and retiring from the world with her elder sister,
devoted herself to prayers for their future happiness.
Then their mother, seeing that she was left alone, aged,
grey-haired and feeble since her two young daughters
had forsaken the world, despairing of any future
happiness, at the age of forty-five shaved her head.

*Sk. Pantchanantarya, i.e. five rebellions. Matricide, par-
ricide, killing an Arhat, causing divisions among the priesthood,
shedding the blood of a Buddha.

Earnestly giving herself up to prayer to Buddha, with her two daughters she sought a happier birth in future.

Thus the spring passed by and the summer grew late; the first winds of autumn began to blow. Gazing at the Milky Way where the lover stars* meet in the heavens, when verses are accustomed to be traced on the leaves of the Kaji,† watching the evening sun hide behind the ridge of the western hills, they likened the sunset to the Pure Land of the West,‡ wondering when they should be reborn in that blessed region and with all desire extinguished abide there for ever.

Thus they continued to meditate on their sad condition, their tears alone being inexhaustible. But one evening when twilight was passing into darkness they had shut their latticed door of bamboo and lighted their dimly burning lamp, and mother and daughters together were repeating the Nembutsu when there came a knocking on the lattice. The three nuns were at once overcome by fear: "Ah! perchance it is some goblin who has come to disturb our prayers and make our Nembutsu of no avail. For what human being will approach a brushwood hut like this by night to which none comes even by day? Such a slight bamboo gate as this, even if we shut it, is easy to break through, therefore let us open it without delay. If indeed it be a pitiless one who will deprive us of life, relying on

---

*Orihime, or the star Vega who is supposed to meet her lover Hikoboshi on the festival of Tanabata, the seventh day of the seventh month. Cf Lafcadio Hearn, The Milky Way.

†Paper-mulberry.

‡Saiho Jodo. Paradise of Amida in the West, from which the Jodo-shu or Pure Land sect derives its name. Sk. Sukhavati.

the True Vow of Amida on whom till now we have called, if we ceaselessly repeat the Nembutsu, surely the Buddha and the attendant Bosatsu will hear our voice and come to meet us, leading us safely to the Paradise of the West." Thus earnestly repeating the Nembutsu, and holding each the hand of the other, they opened wide the bamboo lattice.

But behold it was no evil spirit, but only Hotoke Gozen that stood outside. While Giō was inquiring how Hotoke Gozen had come to visit them, whether in a dream or in her actual person, Hotoke answered amid her tears. "It is a strange thing to speak of what has happened, but if I speak it not, perhaps I may not be remembered. So I will relate all things as they were from the beginning in detail. When first I came to the Court uninvited and was about to go away disappointed after being dismissed, it was at your request that I was called back again; but a woman is a person not to be relied on, so that, not obeying my own conscience, I allowed you to be sent away and even stayed myself in your stead. Now in consequence of this I am overwhelmed with shame and conscience stricken. When I saw you go away I felt it to be through my fault and could not feel at all happy. Moreover when I saw the lines written by your hand on the shōji, 'In autumn meet with the same hapless fate,' I thought it was indeed true. And then when you were once more summoned and when you recited the Imayo verse, the whole matter came to my mind again. But as I did not know where you were, I inquired and heard that you were together in a certain place absorbed in prayer and meditation. Then indeed I felt envious of you, and having zealously begged my freedom since the Lay-priest has no further need of me, when I thought attentively about the matter, the glory of this Shaba-world is a dream of a dream—pleasure and prosperity, of what value are they? Very difficult it is to receive a body and to obtain the mercy of the Buddha. If now I go down in sorrow to the underworld, even though I escape from the endless circle of births and deaths, how difficult will it be to rise up again. In a world of un-certainty for both old and young how can we rely on our youth? The day when the breath enters our body or goes forth we cannot know; our life is more fleeting than gossamer or a flash of lightning; if we boast of the glory that endures for a moment, loss of happiness in the future life must be our portion.

"So this morning stealing out unperceived, I have come hither as you see, putting away my ordinary dress to become a recluse; thus having changed my condition, I entreat that you will condescend to pardon my former trespass, that together repeating the Nembutsu we may sit on one lotus in Paradise together. But if I cannot attain my desire, I will wander away whither I know not, falling down under some tree or on some mossy bank, and ever zealously repeating the Nembutsu, I will strive to attain rebirth in Paradise."

So pressing her sleeve to her face she entreated them. Giō answered her, scarce withholding her tears:—"Not even in a dream did I imagine that you would think thus, while I lived according to the custom of this fleeting world. When I thought of the unhappiness of my condition, often I felt resentment at your conduct in spite of myself, thus suffering loss in this life and the next. But as now you have changed your condition, your former faults have passed away like the dew of morning. Now do I feel extreme happiness knowing that you will without doubt attain your desire and be reborn in bliss. If people may say that my having become a nun was a difficult thing, shall I too so consider it? It was because I hated this world and wished to put an end to my life that I did this. But that you, having no resentment or sorrow, and being now but seventeen years old, should thus despise this world and so earnestly set your mind on the Pure Land, thinking only of the Noble Path, what a happy state of virtuous enlightenment is this indeed!"

So the four of them retired from the world together, morning and evening offering flowers and incense before Buddha's shrine, and with one mind fervently pouring out their petitions; each one sooner or later obtaining her desire for rebirth in bliss. And in the register of the temple Chō-kō-dō built by the Hō-ō Go-Shirakawa the honourable spirits of the four are found enshrined. Indeed it is a very marvellous thing.

THE EXILE OF THE HŌ-Ō

On the twentieth day the forces of the Heike surrounded the Palace of the Hō-ō, and all the ladies-in-waiting and male and female servants, thinking that they would burn the Palace and put all in it to death as Nobuyori had done when he attacked the Sanjo

Palace in Heiji, forgetting all but their own safety,
fled in wild panic without even waiting to garb themselves. Then the former Udaisho, Munemori-no-Kyo,
gave orders to bring the Imperial Car and to make all
haste, whereat the Hō-ō, much perturbed, exclaimed:
"Am I to be banished to some far country or distant
island like Narichika or Shunkwan? I am not aware
of having done anything wrong except perhaps that
since the Emperor is so young I have occasionally given
advice on affairs of state; if however this is not de-
sirable, I will do so no more in future."

Then Jōken Hōin went to Kiyomori at Nishi-
hachijo and urged that, the Hō-ō having gone to the
Toba Palace the night before, it was too severe treatment that he should have not a single person in attendance, so he himself wished to go and attend on His
Majesty. The Nyūdō replied that as he was a trust-
worthy priest he might go; whereupon Jōken was
exceedingly delighted and immediately hastened to the
Toba Palace. Alighting from his car at the entrance,
as soon as he entered within the gate, he heard the
voice of the Hō-ō chanting the Sutras, and it had indeed a very melancholy sound. When the Hōin hastily
entered he saw the Hō-ō sitting and shedding tears
upon the Sutra that he was reading, and in his grief
at the sight, he too pressed the sleeve of his white
costume to his eyes and thus came into his presence
weeping. Only the nun was in attendance. "Ah, Hōin,"
said the Hō-ō, "since you had breakfast yesterday
morning in the Hojuji-den neither last night nor this
morning have you taken any food. Neither have you

slept at all through the night: indeed I fear some danger to your life." The Hōin, controlling his feelings, replied: "Everything in this world has an end; the Heike have held the Empire in their hands for twenty years, but their evil deeds have gone on piling up and verily their end too will come. And surely Tensho-daijin and Sho-Hachimangu will not forget you, while there is also the deity of Hiyoshi on whom you rely, and who will surely vouchsafe his sure protection. The oft-read eight books of the Hokke Sutra will guard you, and then once more the rule will return into your Imperial Power and all the offenders will vanish away like foam on the water." The Hō-ō, on hearing these words was somewhat comforted.

The Emperor was much grieved at the exile of his Prime Minister and the loss of so many of his high officials, but when he heard of the banishment of the Hō-ō to the Toba Palace, he would take no food, and becoming sick, he entered his august sleeping-apart-ment and would not come forth. The ladies-in-wait-ing and the Imperial Consorts were at their wits' end to know what to do. After the Hō-ō had gone to the Toba Palace special worship was held in the Imperial Palace; a dais of mortar* was made in the Seiryōden where the Emperor worshipped Ise-no-Daijingu every night. These prayers were offered for the Hō-ō. The Retired Emperor Nijo was a wise ruler, but since in his opinion an Emperor has neither father nor mother,

---

*It was made under the eaves on the east side of the Seiryoden, one of the halls of the Palace, at the south end; mortar was spread on the boards to obtain the effect of an earthfloor.

he was always opposing the Hō-ō and did not carry on the Imperial Line successfully. Therefore his son the Retired Emperor Rokujō, after having ascended the Throne, unfortunately died on the fourteenth day of the seventh month of the third year of Angen at the age of thirteen.

THE SEINAN DETACHED PALACE

In a hundred volumes we find the saying. "Filial piety is the most important thing. A wise monarch governs the Empire by filial piety." Therefore we see that in China Yao revered his old and feeble mother and Shun respected his obstinate father. It is very blessed when the Imperial Will follows the example of such wise and pious rulers. About this time the Emperor secretly sent this message to the Hō-ō at the Toba Palace: "In such an age even though one live in the Palace what can one do? Perhaps it is best to retire into the mountains and become a recluse as was done by Uda Tenno in the era of Kwampei and by Kwazan Tenno in former times." To this the Hō-ō replied: "Do not think of such a thing. If you remain as you are, it is one source of reliance for me, but if you depart from the Palace, on what can I rely? At any rate wait and see what my fate will be." The Emperor, on receiving this letter, pressed it to his face and wept unrestrainedly.

As the sages have said: "The Emperor is the ship; the subjects are the water. The water may make the ship float well, or again the water may overturn the ship.

The subjects may protect the Emperor, or again the subjects may overthrow the Emperor."* In Hogen and Heiji the Lay-priest Chancellor protected the Emperor, but now in Angen and Jisho he sets him at naught just as the classic says.

The Grand Chancellor Omiya, the Naidaijin Sanjo, the Dainagon Hamuro, and the Chūnagon Nakayama were all dead, and Seirai and Shinhan only were left; but these two, thinking it was no use remaining at Court in such an age, even if they became Dainagon, retired from the world and became monks while still young. Mimbu-Kyō Nyūdō Shinhan having the hoar-frosts of Ohara for company, and Saisho Nyūdō Seirai living among the mists of Kōya, both had no thought for anything but attaining enlightenment in the next existence. In ancient days in China too there were men who hid themselves in the clouds of Shang Shan and cleansed their hearts under the moon of Ying Ch'uan, so what wonder was it that these deeply learned and pure-minded men should forsake so troublesome a world?

When the Saisho Nyūdō among the recesses of Mt Kōya heard that the Emperor also wished to retire from the world, he exclaimed: "Ah, well it was that I have so soon become a recluse; for though to hear of it while here in seclusion is evil enough, how great a grief would it have been to have heard it while in attendance on His Majesty. The revolts of Hogen and Heiji were indeed evil, but now the age has become

*A saying of Confucius.

more degenerate, and such extraordinary things as this have come to pass. What will happen to the Empire in future no one can tell. Would that I could ascend above the clouds or hide myself deep in the farthest mountains." Verily it could not be considered a world in which anyone with any sense would live.

Now the winter was half over and the Hō-ō was in the Seinan Detached Palace. The wind of Yazan sounded shrilly, and the moon shone bright on the frozen garden. The snow fell and piled up on the courtyard, but no one's footsteps were seen upon it. The ice thickened on the ponds, but no flocks of birds resorted thither. The boom of the bell of the great temple resounded in his ears like that of Kuei Ai Ssu in China; the white snow on the western hills reminded him of the scene of the peak of Hsiang Lu. In the cold frosty evening the clink of the fuller's mallet was borne faintly to his pillow; while at dawn he was awakened by the slow wheels creaking on the ice outside the gate. The travellers passing along the highway, the sight of the galloping war-horses, the pomp and movement of this fleeting world, how vain it seems to one who understands. The guards before the Palace gates who kept watch day and night, by what connexion in a former existence was it that they were now brought into this relation with him? What an awe-inspiring thought it was. Thus on every side the Hō-ō found things that gave him pain. So during his exile here he could not help occupying his thoughts with the memory of the various excursions and pilgrimages and festivals he had enjoyed, and the recollection of them would bring tears to his eyes. And so things went on and the fourth year of Jisho began.

Now the second son of the Hō-ō, Prince Mochihito, whose mother was the daughter of Kaga Dainagon Suenari-no-Kyo, was living at the Takakura Palace in Sanjo and so came to be known as Prince Takakura. His Gempuku ceremony had been held secretly when he was fifteen years old, on the fifteenth day of the eleventh month of the first year of Ei-man, at the Omiya Palace at Konoe Kawara. He was known for the elegance of his caligraphy and his brilliant intellect, and might have been Crown Prince and ascended the Throne, but owing to the enmity of the late Empress Ken-shun-mon-in he had to live thus secluded. In springtime he would divert himself by writing poems as he strolled out under the cherry-trees, and in autumn by making exquisite melodies on his flute at the moon-viewing banquets.

While he was thus spending his days, having then reached the age of thirty, in the fourth year of Jisho, Gensammi Nyūdō Yorimasa, who was then living at Konoe Kawara, came secretly to his Palace one evening and spoke his mind to him boldly, thus: "Does your Highness not think it a very miserable thing that you, who are of direct descent in the forty-eighth age from Tensho-daijin,* and the seventy-eighth generation from Jimmu Tenno, and might become Crown Prince and ascend the Throne, should thus live till the age of

---

*Tensho-daijin, the Sun Goddess, Ancestress of the Imperial Family.

thirty in obscurity in this Palace? Quickly raise a revolt and overthrow the Heike!

"Will it not be a most worthy and filial act to relieve the anxiety of the Retired Emperor, repining at his perpetual confinement in the Toba Palace, and to ascend the Throne yourself as Emperor? If your Highness should deign to consider this plan, and issue a Royal Order for its execution, all the many members of the Genji family who are living in the various provinces will gladly flock to your side.

"The two warrior families of Gen and Hei, whose only duty is to quell the enemies of the Throne, have till now been equal in power, but at the present time they are wide asunder as Heaven and Earth; indeed it is not too much to say that their relations are those of servant and master. The provinces are oppressed by the Governors and the fiefs are abused by the commissioners; people are harried in all matters and there is no peace.

"Consider carefully the state of things at present. Outwardly all submit, but inwardly there are none who do not dislike the Heike rule. If therefore Your Highness will agree to issue an Order, the Genji from every province will pour in night and day, and the destruction of the Heike will soon be completed. In that case, though I myself am an old man, I have many young sons and will bring them to fight against the Heike."

The Prince was greatly perplexed to know what to do, so that for some time he did not consent. There was, however, a certain Shonagon Korenaga, who was famous for his skill in physiognomy, so that people called him "Physiognomy Shonagon," and he came and visited the Prince and told him that by his features he was predestined to ascend the Throne, and that therefore he ought not to abandon the attempt to attain his object. Gensammi Nyūdō* also kept on urging him, and suggesting that the plan was an inspiration of Tensho-daijin herself, so that at last he made up his mind to act.

Now on the fifteenth evening of the fifth month, as Prince Takakura was gazing at the beauties of the moon in a cloudy sky, with no thought of anything that might happen, a messenger came post-haste from Yorimasa with a letter, which his foster brother Rokujo-no-Suke-no-Daiyu Munenobu at once brought to him. It ran thus: "The plot is already revealed, and you are to be banished to Tosa: the officials of the Kebiishi have orders to take you, so leave the Palace quickly and go to Miidera. I myself am shortly coming to the Capital."

The Prince was dumbfounded at this news, and at a loss how to act, when one of his samurai who was always in attendance on him, Chōhyōye-no-Jō Hasebe Nobutsura by name, spoke out saying: "There is nothing difficult in that; it is easy to escape in woman's attire." This counsel seemed good, so the Prince let his hair loose, donned a female costume, and put on his head a wide straw hat such as the townswomen wear, while Rokujo-no-Suke-no-Daiyu Munenobu went with him

---

*A retired man who has nominally become a Buddhist monk. Lit. "One who has entered the Way" (of Buddha).

to carry his umbrella, and a youth named Tsuru Maru accompanied them, carrying some articles in a bag on his head. Thus imitating the appearance of a young retainer escorting his mistress, they slipped out of the Palace toward the north.

TAKAKURA-NO-MIYA GOES TO ONJOJI.

Thus Prince Takakura, leaving Takakura on the north and Konoe on the east, crossed the river Kamo and proceeded to enter Nyoiyama. Formerly the Tenno of Kiyomihara, when attacked by Prince Otomo, went to Yoshinoyama in the guise of a woman, and this Prince was now in just such a plight, fleeing far away through the trackless and unknown hills the whole night through; his feet, torn and bleeding through the unaccustomed toil, stained the sand like the dark maple leaves, and it must have seemed that the dew of the moist verdure was overwhelmed by his tears. Thus they reached Miidera at morning light, and when the priests heard His Highness had come to seek refuge with them, to save, it might be, his fleeting life, they were exceeding respectfully overjoyed, and appointing the Hō-rin-in as his lodging, gave him food and clothing with due ceremony.

Then the Prince, seeing that Hieizan had turned against them, and Nara had not yet sent their men, since Miidera alone could do nothing, on the twenty-third day of the same month left that temple and started for the Southern Capital. The Prince had with him two flutes of Chinese bamboo called "Semi-

ori" and "Koeda." Of these Semiori was made of
a bamboo with joints like a living Cicada (Semi),
which had been sent from China as a return gift when
in the reign of Toba-in much gold-dust had been sent
as a present to the Emperor of the Sung dynasty.
Wondering how such a rare treasure could be well
carved, it had been sent to Daisei-in-no-Sōjō Kakusō
of Miidera and placed on the altar while prayer was
offered for seven days, after which it was carved. On
one occasion Takamatsu-no-Chūnagon Sanehira-no-
Kyo came to the temple and played on it, but forgetting it was no ordinary flute, he dropped it to the
ground from his knees, and the flute, feeling the reproach, broke at the joint like a Semi; so that ever
after it was called Semiori. As the Prince excelled
so greatly at flute-playing he had inherited it. But now,
thinking that his end was nigh, he deposited it in the
Kondo Hall before Miroku Bosatsu.

The Fight at the Bridge

Now the Prince fell from his horse six times between
Uji and Miidera, because he had no sleep the previous
night, so they tore up about six yards of the planking
of the bridge at Uji and he entered the temple of
Byōdō-in and rested there awhile. The men of Rokuhara, learning that he was fleeing to Nara, at once
started off in pursuit to take him and put him to
death. Crossing over Kobatayama, about twenty-eight
thousand men in all, they pressed on to the bridge-head
of Uji. Perceiving that the enemy were at Byōdō-in,

The fight at Uji bridge.

they raised their war-cry three times, when they were
answered by that of the Prince's men. The vanguard,
seeing the danger, raised a cry of alarm: "Take care!
they have torn up the bridge!" But the rearguard paid
no heed and pushed them on with cries of "Advance!
Advance!" so that some two hundred horsemen of the
leading company fell through into the river and
perished in the stream.

Then the warriors of both sides, taking their stand
at each end of the bridge, began a duel of archery, and
on the side of the Prince, Oya-no-Shuncho, Gochiin-
no-Tajima, Watanabe-no-Habuku, Sazuku, and Tsuzu-
ku-no-Genda shot so powerfully that their shafts
pierced the enemy through both shield and armour.
Gensammi Nyūdō Yorimasa, knowing in his heart that
this fight would be his last, went forth in a suit of
armour of blue-and-white spots worn over his long-
sleeved Court hitatare, purposely wearing no helmet on
his head, while his son Izu-no-kami Nakatsuna wore a
suit of black armour over a hitatare of red brocade, he
also leaving his head bare for greater ease in drawing
the bow.

Then Gochiin-no-Tajima, throwing away the sheath
of his long halberd, strode forth alone on to the bridge,
whereupon the Heike straightway shot at him fast and
furious. Tajima, not at all perturbed, ducking to avoid
the higher ones and leaping up over those that flew low,
cut through those that flew straight with his whirring
halberd, so that even the enemy looked on in admiration. Thus it was that he was dubbed "Tajima the
arrow cutter."

Another of the soldier-priests, Tsutsui-no-Jōmyō Meishu, wearing armour laced with black leather over a hitatare of dyed cloth, and a helmet of five plates, a sword in a black lacquered sheath at his side and a quiver of twenty-four black feathered arrows on his back, his bow being also of black lacquer, gripping his favourite white-handled halberd in his hand, also sprang forward alone on to the bridge and shouted in a mighty voice: "Let those at a distance listen, those that are near can see; I am Tsutsui Jōmyō Meishu, the priest; who is there in Miidera who does not know me, a warrior worth a thousand men? Come on anyone who thinks himself some one, and we will see!"

And loosing off his twenty-four arrows like lightning-flashes he slew twelve of the Heike soldiers and wounded eleven more. One arrow yet remained in his quiver, but, flinging away his bow, he stripped off his quiver and threw that after it, cast off his foot-gear, and springing barefoot on to the beams of the bridge, he strode across. All were afraid to cross over, but he walked the broken bridge as one who walks along the street Ichijo or Nijo of the Capital. With his naginata he mows down five of the enemy, but with the sixth the halberd snaps asunder in the midst and flinging it away he draws his sword, wielding it in the zigzag style, the interlacing, cross, reversed dragon-fly, waterwheel, and eight-sides-at-once styles of fencing, and cutting down eight men; but as he brought down the ninth with an exceeding mighty blow on the helmet, the blade snapped at the hilt and fell splash into the water beneath. Then seizing his dirk which was the only weapon he had left, he plied it as one in the death fury.

Now a retainer of Ajari Kyōshu, Ichirai Hoshi by name, a man of great strength and courage, was fighting behind Jōmyō, but as the beams were so narrow he could not come alongside him, so placing a hand on the neckpiece of his helmet, he shouted: "Pardon me Jōmyō, this is no good," and springing over his shoulder to the front fought mightily until he fell. Ichirai Hoshi being killed, Jōmyō crawled back again and retired to the Byōdō-in, where he sat down on the grass before the gate, and stripping off his armour, counted the dints of the arrows that had struck him.

There were sixty-three in all, but of these only five had pierced through, and none of the wounds being very severe, he treated them with cautery; then, covering his head and changing his clothes, using his broken bow as a staff he went down on foot to Nara. Following the example of Jōmyō the soldier monks of Mii-dera with the Watanabe clan of Gensammi Nyūdō's men vied with each other in pressing forward over the beams of the bridge, and fought till sundown, some returning victorious, and some, after being wounded, cutting themselves open and jumping into the river.

Then the commander of the samurai, Kazusa-no-kami Tadakiyo, came to the commander-in-chief of the Heike forces: "See here," he said "the battle on the bridge is very fierce; we ought to ford the river, but after the rains of the fifth month neither man nor horse can live in the stream; shall we go round by Yodo, Moarai, or Kawachiji? What is to be done?"

Then Ashikaga Matataro Tadatsuna, a young man in his eighteenth year, spoke saying: "Why not leave the samurai of India or China to go to Yodo, Moarai or Kawachiji, for that is not our way. If we don't rout the enemy that confront us here, the Prince will get away to Nara, and then you will have all the forces of Yoshino and Totsugawa to deal with and that will be no light affair. On the boundary of Musashi and Kozuke there is a great river called the Tonegawa, and there the Ashikaga and the Chichibu are always fighting each other, and on one occasion, when the front were attacking at Nagai ford and the rear at Koga-sugi ford, a certain Nitta Nyūdō of Kozuke, who was coming to the help of the Ashikaga from the Sugi ford, being told by them that the Chichibu had destroyed all the boats that had been provided to cross, exclaimed: "If we do not ford the river here it will be a disgrace to our reputation as samurai; to be drowned is but to die. Forward then!" and using their horses as a raft they forded the river.

As the samurai of the East Country say: "Keep your face to the enemy, and when separated by a river, shun the swift rapids by the bank. This river is neither more nor less swift and deep than the Tonegawa, so come along sirs," and he plunged into the stream. Ogo, Omuro, Fukasu, Yamakami, Nawa-no-Taro, Sanuki, Hirotsuna, Shirodaiyu, Onodera-no-Zenji Taro, Heyako-no-Shiro, and among the younger men Ubukata-no-jiro, Kirifu-no-Rokuro, and Tanaka-no-Sota immediately dashed in after him with some three hundred men behind them, shouting the Ashikaga war-cry.

"Put the heads of the weaker horses downstream, those of the stronger upstream!" he shouted. "If the horses keep their feet give them the rein and let them walk, but if they get off their feet let them have their heads and swim them; if you are washed downstream stick the butt of your bow down into the bottom; join hands and go across in line; if your horse's head gets down pull it up, but don't pull it up too far or you will fall off backwards; sit tight in the saddle and keep your feet firm in the stirrups. Where the water is slow and deep get up over the horse's tail; don't shoot while in the water; if the enemy shoots don't draw bow in return; keep your head down and your neck-piece well sloped upwards, but not too far or you will be shot in the crown of the helmet; be light on the horse and firm against the stream; don't go straight across or you will be washed away, keep obliquely to the stream." Thus advising and encouraging them he brought the whole three hundred rapidly across without losing a man.

THE FATE OF THE PRINCE

Then Ashikaga Matataro, wearing armour with red leather lacing over a hitatare of russet-gold brocade, with a helmet ornamented with lofty horns, a gold-mounted tachi by his side, and twenty-four black-and-white spotted arrows on his back, carrying a black lacquered bow lashed with red bands, and riding on a

light-brown horse with a gold-mounted saddle on which
was the crest of an owl on an oak bough, stood up in
his stirrups and shouted loudly: "I am Ashikaga Matataro Takatsuna, aged seventeen, son of Ashikaga Taro
Toshitsuna of Shimotsuke, descended in the tenth
generation from Tawara Toda Hidesato, the renowned
warrior who gained great fame and reward for destroying Masakado the enemy of the Emperor, and
though it may be at the risk of divine anger that one
without rank or office should draw bow against a
Prince of the Royal House, yet as I owe deep gratitude to the Heike for many favours, here I stand to
meet any on the side of Gensammi Nyūdō who dares
to face me." And he made an onset and fought his
way within the gate of the Byōdō-in.

Then the commander Sahyoye-no-kami Tomomori,
seeing this, ordered his forces to cross over, and about
twenty-eight thousand horsemen plunged into the river,
so that the rapids of the Ujigawa were dammed and
stayed by the mass of men and horses, and the foot-
soldiers crossing below the horsemen were hardly
wetted above their knees. But everything is carried
away by the natural force of water, so the men of
Ise and Iga, to the number of six hundred horsemen,
were washed away through their ranks being broken
by the force of the current, and their armour of various
hues, green, scarlet and red, rose and sank as they
were swept away, like the maple leaves on Kannabi-
yama, when in late autumn they are blown by the moun-

tain blasts into the Tatsuta river and collect in masses
where the flood is dammed.

Among them three gallants, clad in the scarlet
armour of a leader of armies, stuck helplessly in a
fish decoy, and Izu-no-kami, watching them as they
struggled in the rapids, composed this stanza:

> See the Ise braves
> All in scarlet armour bright,
> What a gallant show!
> Uji's decoys hold them fast
> Like a lot of frozen fish!

They were Kuroda-no-Gohei Shiro, Hino-no-Juro
and Otobe-no-Yashichi, all men of Ise, and Hino-no-
Juro, a veteran soldier, wedging the butt of his bow
into a cleft of the rock, scrambled out by its aid and then
pulled out his two companions, thus saving their lives.

Now when the whole force had reached the other side
they advanced and fought their way in through the gate
of the Byōdō-in and in the confusion the Prince
attempted to escape toward Nara, while Gensammi's
men the Watanabe and the warrior priests of Miidera
strove to hold back the foe with their bows and arrows.
The veteran warrior Gensammi, now more than three
score years and ten, was soon wounded in the right
elbow by an arrow and was about to retire within the
temple to die calmly by his own hand, when a band of
the enemy threw themselves in his way, whereupon
his second son Gendaiyu-no-Hangwan Kanetsuna
turned to counter them and let his father escape.

His armour laced with Chinese silk was worn over a
hitatare of dark blue brocade, and he rode a cream

coloured horse with a saddle mounted in gold. Then
Kazusa-no-Taro Hangwan shot an arrow that struck
him beneath the helmet, and as he staggered at the
blow, Kazusa-no-kami's son Jiro Maru, a strong and
valiant fighter, clad in green armour with a helmet of
three plates on his head, unsheathed his sword and
sprang upon him.

They both grappled immediately and fell together,
when Gendaiyu-Hangwan, who was a powerful man,
gripped Jiro Maru, pressed him down and cut off his
head, but just then fourteen or fifteen of the Heike
horsemen came up and Kanetsuna was overpowered
at last by numbers and slain.　Izu-no-kami Nakatsuna too, after fighting with reckless bravery, covered
with wounds, retired to the Tsuridono of the Byōdō-
in and there put an end to himself, his head being taken
up by Shimokawabe-no-Tosaburo Kiyochika and thrown
under the veranda.

Gensammi Nyūdō Yorimasa, calling Watanabe
Choshichi Tonau, bade him strike off his head, but he
refused, overcome by the thought of cutting off his
master's head while alive, but offered to do so after
he had committed suicide.　Then Gensammi Nyūdō,
turning to the West, put his hands together and repeated the Nembutsu ten times in a loud voice, after
which he composed this sad stanza ;

> Like a fossil tree
> On which never flower grows
> Even so am I.
> Sad indeed has been my life
> Without any hope of fruit.

The death of Minamoto Yorimasa.

And with these last words he thrust the point of his sword into his belly, and bowing his face to the ground pierced himself through and died. It was not a time when people usually make poems, but as he had been extremely fond of this pastime from his youth up, so even at the hour of death he did not forget it. Choshichi Tonau took his head, and fastening stones to it sunk it in a deep part of the Ujigawa.

Now Hida-no-kami Kageie, a veteran soldier, suspecting that Prince would certainly attempt to flee to Nara under cover of the fighting, rode hard on his track with four or five hundred men in full armour, and as he expected, overtook him in front of the torii of Kōmyōzan with his escort of about thirty horsemen. As the arrows flew like rain no one could tell whose it was, but one of the arrows of the Heike struck the Prince in the side so that he fell from his horse, whereupon they killed him and cut off his head.

Oni Sado, Aratosa, Kodaiyu, and Gyobu-no-Shunshu who accompanied him, not wishing to live after their master, threw themselves upon the enemy and died fighting together. Among them his foster-brother, Rokujo-no-suke no Taiyu Munenobu, jumped into the pond at Niino, and hiding his face among the waterweed, lay there trembling. Soon after the Heike came riding back again to the number of four or five hundred horsemen, laughing and shouting as they rode, and peeping out he could see in the midst of them a headless corpse in white clothing borne on a shutter. It was the Prince without doubt, for in his girdle was the flute "Koeda" which he had bidden them bury with him in the coffin if he died. He earnestly wished to rush out and throw himself on the body, but fear restrained him, and after the enemy had all passed by he came out of the pond, and wringing out his wet garments returned weeping to the Capital, where there was none who did not hold him in aversion.

Now about seven thousand soldier-priests of Nara in full armour had gone forth to meet the Prince, and while the vanguard reached as far as Kōzu and the rearguard was still surging out of the southern gate of the Kōfukuji, they heard that the Prince had been slain before the torii of Kōmyōzan, alas! but fifty cho distant from Kōzu. So, unable to do any more, they halted, lamenting that they had not come up in time.

The August Lying-in of the Empress Kenrei-mon-in

Now from the hour of the Tiger (4 a.m.) on the twelfth day of the eleventh month of the same year the Empress began to be in travail, and Rokuhara and all the Capital were in an uproar. The place of lying-in was the Ikedono mansion at Rokuhara and the Hō-ō himself made an august visit of ceremony: after him all the Courtiers from the Kwampaku and Dajo-daijin downwards, every one who could be considered anyone at all, and every one without exception who held emoluments or office and hoped for place and promotion in future, came and presented themselves at Rokuhara.

When we refer to former cases of the lying-in of Consorts and Empresses there was always a great pardon. On the first day of the ninth month of the second year of Daiji, when Tai-ken-mon-in was brought to bed, a great pardon was proclaimed, and on this occasion things were done according to that precedent and a very extensive pardon was issued, so that among those guilty of serious offences Shunkwan Sōzu was unhappily the only one who did not share in it. A vow was made that there should be an Imperial Progress of the Empress and Crown Prince to the shrines of Hachiman, Hirano, and Oharano if the birth was easy and a prince was born. This vow Sengen Hōin respectfully heard: we speak of it with reverence.

Prayer was also made at twenty shrines of the Kami beginning with Ise Daimyojin, and the Sutras were read at the temples of Tōdaiji and Kōfukuji beside sixteen others, those who read the Sutras being chosen officials among those who served the shrines. Retainers wearing kariginu of ornamented brocade and girt with swords walked in procession, carrying various sacred vessels and the Imperial Sword and The Imperial Vesture, crossing over from the Higashi-no-dai to the southern court and going forth from the middle-gate. A most auspicious and beautiful scene.

Taira Shigemori as was natural to his calm and unmoved nature, came long after the others with his eldest son Koremori and many nobles of lesser rank in a procession of cars bringing presents; forty changes of garments of various kinds, seven silver ornamented swords borne upon large trays, and twelve horses. Shigemori was the elder brother of the Empress and since his relation was especially paternal there was reason why he should send these horses.

Gojo-no-Dainagon Kunitsuna also sent two horses, and people wondered if this was because of his great desire for a prince to be born or because of his great virtue. Moreover horses were presented to seventy shrines from Ise even to Itsukushima in Aki, and very many sets of decorations for the horses in the Imperial Stables.

The Lord Abbot of Ninnaji, Shukaku Hō-Shinno, read the Kujaku Sutra, while the Tendai Zasshu Kakukai Hō-Shinno chanted the Sutra of the Seven Buddhas. The Lord Abbot of Miidera, Enkei Shinno, chanted the Sutra of Kongo Doji, beside which Godaikokuzo, the Six Kwannon, the Ichiji Kinrin Godan Sutra, Rokuji Karin, Hachiji Monju, and the Fugen of long life were all invoked and recited from beginning to end. The smoke of incense filled the whole Palace and the sound of bells echoed to heaven, while the sonorous chanting of the Sutras made men's hair stand up. Whatever evil spirits there might be, and in whatever direction they might turn, they were put to flight. Then too a life-size statue of Yakushi Nyorai and the Five Wondrous Kings* was begun for the chapel of Buddha.

Now though all these things were done and the pains came continually upon the Empress, yet she was not quickly delivered, and Kiyomori and the Nii Dono his

*Fudo Myo-o, Kosanse Myo-o, Gunchari Yasha Myo-o, Taiitoku Myo-o, Kongo Yasha Myo-o.

consort, pressing their hands to their breasts in perplexity, continually ejaculated: "What is to be done? What shall we do?" And whenever anyone inquired something of them, all they replied was: "Do as you please. Do as you like:" the Lay-priest adding, "Ah, if I were with my army in the field I should not feel anxiety like this."

All the while the diviners, the two Sōjō, Hokaku and Shō-un, Shunkei Hōin, and the two Sōzu, Kōzen and Jissen, were chanting the Sutras and incessantly telling their rosaries and praying, invoking the Three Treasures of their temples and all their ancient and venerated statues and books and holy pictures. Indeed it was a most blessed sight. And amid all this sanctification, the Hō-ō, who was just at this time engaged in purification ceremonies preparatory to making a pilgrimage to Kumano, sat in a chamber near the brocade curtain behind which the Empress was, and recited the Sutra of Kwannon of the Thousand Hands.

Now at this moment a change came. Though the holy mediums who were wildly dancing went into a trance, for some time they were silent. "Ah," quoth the Hō-ō, "whatever evil spirit there may be, how can it come near when I am present? Beside which all these hostile influences have been granted Our Imperial Benevolence and restored to mankind, and even though they are not grateful yet how can they now hinder us? Let them quickly be put to flight!" (When women have difficult labour and there is some obstacle hindering them, however troublesome and difficult it may be, if a mighty spell be chanted earnestly then the demon will depart and the birth become easy and successful.)

So they all applied themselves diligently to their crystal rosaries with the result that not only was the Imperial Consort safely delivered but a Prince was born. Then Hon-Sammi Chūjō Shigehira, who was then acting as Chugu-no-Suke, came forth from behind the curtain and announced in a loud voice: "The august labour is safely ended and a Prince has deigned to be born."

The Hō-ō was the first to offer his congratulations; then the Kwampaku Matsu Dono and the Dajo-daijin and all the courtiers below him and all the assistants and acolytes, the chief astrologers, chief physicians, and all the diviners high and low, shouted aloud their joy in concert so that the sound reverberated even to without the gates and did not subside for some while. The Nyūdō too, in the excess of his joy, lifted up his voice and wept: these were tears of joy indeed.

Komatsu Dono immediately hurried to the Palace of the Empress bringing ninety-nine mon in coin to place beside the pillow of the baby Prince saying: "Heaven is father and Earth is mother. May your life be as long as that of the magician Tung Fang Sō: may your mind be as that of the Sun Goddess." And taking a bow of mulberry and six arrows of "Artemisia," he shot them toward heaven and earth and the four-quarters of the world.

There were many things that people thought laughable in the lying-in of the Empress. For instance, the Hō-ō acting as a soothsayer; and in the second place, as it is the custom at the lying-in of an Imperial Consort that a rice-vessel (koshiki*) should be rolled down from the ridge of the Palace roof, if a Prince is born it is to be rolled down the south side, and if a Princess, down the north side,† this was done as usual; but by mistake it was rolled down the north side, whereat there was a great uproar, and it was brought up again and rolled down once more in the proper manner. This was an ill-omened event in the opinion of most people. What appeared ridiculous was the flurry and agitation of the Lay-priest Chancellor, in contrast to the conduct of Shigemori, which was much admired.

Then came seven astrologers to perform a thousand exorcisms, and among them was an old man named Kamon-no-kami Tokiharu. He was a man of small property and office, and as so many people came thronging there like the bamboo-shoots that stand thick together, yea even like rice sprouts, flax, bamboos and reeds, he cried out: "I am an official. Make way!" and pressing through the midst of the crowd, what a sight

---

*cf. Sansom's note on Tsurezure Gusa, p. 46. Explaining the custom the Tsurezure Gusa says: "In the case of a birth, in the Imperial Family the dropping of a 'koshiki' is not a fixed custom but is a charm used when the afterbirth is obstructed. When it is not obstructed this is not done. The custom came from the common people and has no authority. The 'koshiki' used are brought from the village of Ohara. In pictures treasured from ancient times one sees the dropping of these rice-vessels shown when a birth has taken place among the common people." The charm originates in the assonance of koshiki, rice-box, and koshi-ki, pain in the loins. The name of Ohara (also=great belly) is also significant.

†The quarter of the women's apartments. Cf. Kita-no-kata.

he presented! Having trodden off his right shoe, he
was resting for a moment when his head-dress also got
knocked off, and at such a time to see a dignified old
man in ceremonial court costume, with his hair in disorder, pacing along, was more than the younger
courtiers were able to endure, and they burst forth into
uncontrollable mirth.   For the astrologers say that
their peculiar gait must be most punctiliously observed.
A strange thing too was that he knew nothing about
it all at the time, though afterwards when he came to
think about it he remembered everything.

Nue

Now Gensammi Nyūdō Yorimasa was the fifth
generation from Settsu-no-kami Raiko, the grandson
of Mikawa-no-kami Yoritsuna and son of Hyogo-no-
kami Nakamasa. At the time of the fight of Hōgen he
was on the side of the Imperial Army, but received
no reward: also in the rebellion of Heiji he forsook all
his kinsmen and fought on the same side, but his re-
compense was small. For long he only held the title of
Guard of the Palace, and had not the privilege of entry
to Court, but after he was old he obtained the privilege
by composing the following verse:

> No one looks my way
> As I stand a faithful guard
> At the Palace Gate.
> How am I to view the moon
> In the shadow of the trees?

For this he was granted the lower grade of the Upper
Fourth Rank, and so he remained for some time until,

wishing to proceed to the Third Rank, he made another stanza, thus:

> So I go through life,
> Picking up acorns* that fall
> Underneath the oak.
> I have now but little hope
> Of a rise to higher things.

Some time afterwards he retired from the world and was known as Gensammi Nyūdō Yorimasa (Minamoto Third Rank), being seventy-five the same year. Among the many deeds of renown that Yorimasa performed in the course of his life the most remarkable was in the Ninpei period when the Emperor Konoe-in was on the Throne. Every night the Emperor was frightened by something, and though he summoned the most celebrated of the priests and had them chant those Sutras most potent for exorcism it was all of no effect. The time that the Emperor was thus troubled was about the hour of the Ox (2 a.m.), when a black cloudy mass used to come up from the direction of the wood of Higashi Sanjo and hover over the Palace, and it always affrighted him. So a Council of Courtiers was held about it. Now in former days in the period of Kwanji, when Horikawa-in was on the Throne, this Emperor was terrified in the very same way, and Yoshiie Ason, who was Commander of the Guards at that time, took up his position on the veranda of the Shishinden, and at the usual time of the apparition twanged his bow-string three times and declaimed in a loud and terrible voice: "I am Minamoto Yoshiie

---

*The Japanese word "shii" means both "acorn" and "Fourth Rank."

formerly Mutsu-no-kami," so that the hair of those
that heard it stood on end, whereat the distress of His
Majesty was relieved. So according to this precedent
Yorimasa was chosen from among the warriors of the
Taira and Minamoto families. He was at this time
only Hyoye-no-kami, and on being informed of it he
said. "From former times samurai have been stationed
at the Palace to drive away rebels and to smite those
who disobey the Imperial Commands, but it is the first
time that I have ever heard of their having apparitions
to deal with." But as it was an Imperial Order he
went. He took with him his most trusted retainer I-
no-Hayata of Tōtōmi, who carried an arrow feathered
with the underfeathers of an eagle's wing, while he
himself, wearing a double kariginu, carried his lacquered bow and two barbed arrows and proceeded to
the veranda of the Shishinden. The reason for his
taking two arrows was that one Masayori-no-Kyo, who
was at that time Sashoben, had suggested that he be
chosen to deal with the monster, and so Yorimasa had
determined that if he failed to hit the creature with the
one arrow he would shoot the other straight at Masa-
yori's neck. After a while, as has been described, at
the time when the Emperor was always wont to be
alarmed, a mass of black cloud came from the direction
of the wood by Higashi Sanjo and floated over the top
of the Palace. Yorimasa, looking up, saw a strange
shape in the midst of the cloud and determining not to
live if he missed, took an arrow, and earnestly repeating in his heart the invocation to the god of war,
"Namu Hachiman Dai-Bosatsu!" drew the bow

mightily and let fly. The arrow flew straight to the
mark and Yorimasa gave a loud shout of triumph as
I-no-Hayata came running up, seized the thing as it
fell and, pressing it down with might and main, pierced
it through nine times with his sword. Then many
others ran up with torches, and when they came to inspect it they found it was a most horrible monster with
a monkey's head, the body of a badger, the tail of a
snake and feet like a tiger, its voice being like a Nue
bird. The Emperor, out of his great gratitude to Yorimasa, presented him with a famous sword called
"Shishio" or Lion King. This was handed to the
Sadaijin Yorinaga to give to Yorimasa, and as His
Excellency proceeded to come half-way down the steps
of the Palace, it being then the tenth day of the fourth
month, the voice of a cuckoo that chanced to fly over-
head echoed twice or thrice, whereupon the Sadaijin
exclaimed:

> See the cuckoo, too,
> Wishes to make known your fame
> Far beyond the clouds.

But Yorimasa, sticking out his right knee and spread-
ing out his left sleeve, looked up at the crescent moon
in the sky and replied:

> 'Tis the moon you have to thank,
> I but let the arrow fly.

Then he received the sword and retired.

This Yorimasa, beside being a peerless warrior, was
also a distinguished poet and much admired by his
contemporaries. The Nue they put into a boat and set
it adrift. In the period Oho also, in the reign of Nijo-

in a monstrous bird called Nue was heard to cry in the Palace, so that the heart of the Emperor was troubled, and so as had been done before he summoned Yorimasa. It was the evening of the twentieth day of the fifth month. The Nue only flew once over the Palace and its voice was not heard a second time. It was so dark that nothing could be seen and therefore there was nowhere to aim, so Yorimasa took a great whirring arrow, and shot it over the roof of the Palace at the place where the cry had been heard. The Nue, alarmed at the sound of the arrow, sprang up into the sky, when Yorimasa, quickly seizing a smaller whirring arrow, let it fly. It struck and brought down the creature, whereupon all those in the Palace came rushing out shouting confusedly. On this occasion Yorimasa received a robe of honour from the Emperor. This time it was Oi-no-Mikado no Udaijin Kinyoshi who received it to present to Yorimasa. "In ancient China," said he in admiration, "Yang Yu shot a wild goose beyond the clouds, but now Yorimasa has shot a Nue in the rain:

> Even in the dark
> In the rainy days of spring
> You have hit the mark."

> "Nay, it was not such a feat,
> For, I think, 'twas twilight still."

replied Yorimasa as he received the robe and retired. Then, having received the fief of Izu, he appointed his eldest son Nakatsuna as its Governor, and having attained the Third Rank was living at ease on his estates in Tamba and Wakasa, when he started this vain revolt and perished with the Prince and his sons and grandsons.

MOON-VIEWING

The ninth day of the sixth month was fixed for the commencement of the new Palace, the tenth day of the eighth month for the celebration of the raising of the roof-beams and the thirteenth day of the eleventh month for the Imperial Entry. The Ancient Capital was now falling into ruin, but the new one was full of life and bustle. Thus sadly did the summer pass and the autumn had already come on. When the autumn was almost half over, those who were in the new capital of Fukuhara went out to the places famous for moon-viewing. Some went along the shore from Suma to Akashi, recalling the ancient memories of the romance of Prince Genji, and some crossed over the strait to the Isle of Awaji to gaze at the moon at Eji-maga-iso. Others made their way to Shiraura, Fuki-age, Waka-no-Ura, Sumiyoshi, Naniwa, Takasago, or Onoe and stayed to view the moon at dawn before returning. Those who had stayed behind in the Ancient Capital went to Hirosawa at Fushimi for moon-viewing.

Now Tokudaiji-no-Sadaisho Sanesada, being greatly devoted to the moonlight scenery of the Ancient Capital, after the tenth day of the eighth month went up thither from Fukuhara. Ah! how changed did he find everything. Before the front gates of the few remaining houses the grass had grown thickly, and in the dew-laden courts was a tall undergrowth of mugwort and rushes, while the chirp of the insects shrilled everywhere, and the chrysanthemum and purple orchid grew wild as in the plains. Only the Omiya Palace at Konoe

Kawara still recalled the grandeur of former days. The Sadaisho proceeded to this Palace with his retainers and knocked at the outer gate. From within the voice of a woman called reproachfully. "Who is it that brushes the dew from the weeds of such a neglected place?" "It is Sanesada who has come up from Fukuhara," was the reply. "Ah, in that case, since the great gate is locked, I pray you enter by the postern on the eastern side," she answered. So the Taisho entered by the eastern postern. Now the occupant of the Palace, the Senior Dowager Empress, Consort of Konoe Tenno, finding time hang heavy on her hands, had opened the lattice on the south side of her apartment and was solacing herself by playing on the Biwa, reviving the while her memories of former days, when unexpectedly the Sadaisho entered. His appearance greatly surprised the Empress, who laid aside her Biwa and exclaimed: "Ah! is it indeed reality or am I in a dream? But pray enter." In the volume of the Genji Monogatari called "Uji" it is written how the daughter of the Lay-devotee Prince, oppressed with melancholy at the passing of autumn, spent the night playing the Biwa to calm her troubled spirit, and becoming impatient at last for the moon of dawn to appear, her feelings overcame her and she beckoned to it with the plectrum of her Biwa. By this we can understand something of the Empress's feelings.

Now in this Palace was a waiting damsel who went by the name of "Eve-awaiting Maid," and the reason of this nick-name was that once the Empress had asked which was the most affecting, the awaiting a lover in

the evening or the parting from him in the morning,
and the girl had replied with the verse:

> When at eve we wait
> And the lover does not come,
> Then the temple bell
> Sadder sounds than does the crow
> Of the cock that bids us part.

Calling this lady, Sanesada-no-Kyo conversed with her
about many things past and present, and then he made
the following song in the Imayo style about the ruined
state of the former capital:

> When we now view the Capital of yore,
> How is it wasted like a reed-grown plain!
> Through all its chambers pours the moon's pale light;
> The blasts of autumn pierce me to the bone.

This strain he sang three times clearly, and the
Empress and all her lady-attendants were so moved
that they buried their faces in their sleeves and wept.

Meanwhile the dawn broke and the Sadaisho took
leave of them and returned to Fukuhara. On the way
he called a certain Kurando of his company and said
to him: "I think that lady-in-waiting seemed very
much pained at parting, I pray you go back and say
something suitable to the occasion." So the Kurando
hurried back again at his bidding, and improvising this
stanza, recited it to her as though from his lord:

> Though you said 'tis nought—
> That cock-crow at early dawn
> Hastening your love—
> This time, so I like to think
> You look rather desolate.

The lady at once replied in the following lines:

> Though the bell at eve,
> When we wait in vain for him,
> Is a painful sound,
> How I hate the cock-crow now
> Heralding the time to part!

Then the Kurando hastened back again and related the whole affair to his lord, whereat the Sadaisho praised him saying that it was well said indeed; and ever after this Kurando was known as "Mono-ka-wa-no-kurando," after the first words of his poem.

THE AUSTERITIES OF MONGAKU

Now Minamoto Yoritomo had been spared and banished to Hiru-ga-kojima in Izu in the domain of Hōjō on the twentieth day of the third month of the first year of Eiryaku only through the urgent pleading of the late Ike-no-zenni, when his father Sama-no-kami Yoshitomo was executed in the twelfth month of the first year of Heiji for the rebellion that he made. He was at that time fourteen years of age, and having spent some twenty autumns in exile was now of mature years; and if one should wonder why he stirred up a revolt in this year, it was because of the exhortation of Mongaku Shonin of Takao.

This Mongaku was formerly known as Endo Musha Morito and was the son of Watanabe Mochito, having been a retainer of Josei-mon-in, a consort of Toba-in, but at the age of nineteen, possessed by a desire to enter the Way of Buddha, he shaved his head and started to practise mortification of the flesh. With the intention of proving how much he could endure, he stripped himself naked and lay down on his back in a bamboo thicket in the depth of the mountains under the scorching sun during the hottest days of the sixth month, when there was no breath of wind, and the horse-flies and mosquitoes and wild bees and ants and every kind of poisonous insect came and settled on his body and bit and stung him, but in spite of this he did not move a muscle.

Thus he remained for the space of seven days, but on the eighth day he arose and asked whether religious asceticism demanded as much as this or not. "If it were so severe" was the reply, "how could people survive it?" Thus reassured, he began his austere life by going to Kumano, intending to live in retirement at Nachi. Now at Nachi is a famous waterfall, and Mongaku determined to bathe in it as a religious exercise. It was past the tenth day of the twelfth month when he arrived there and the snow had fallen thickly; the river that ran through the valley was silent in its icy shroud; the freezing blasts blew fiercely from the mountain-tops and the waterfall was a mass of crystal icicles, while the twigs were everywhere hidden under their heavy coat of snow.

Mongaku, invoking the magic power of Fudo Myō-ō, immersed himself up to the neck in the pool of the waterfall and remained thus two, three, then four days, but on the fifth, unable to endure any longer, losing his senses he was washed away by the mighty volume of the falling water, and carried some six or seven hundred yards downstream, his body dashing against the sharp-edged rocks as it rose and fell in the swirling current.

Then suddenly there appeared a beautiful boy who seized his hand and drew him safely up on to the bank. The bystanders, seeing his dangerous plight, soon kindled a fire and warmed him so that he recovered consciousness, for it was not his fate to perish, but as soon as he again drew his breath and opened his eyes, he glared about him in great anger, crying out with a loud voice: "I am under a vow to stand under the waterfall for thrice seven days and repeat the magic invocation of Fudo three hundred thousand times, and to-day being only the fifth day, who has dared to pull me out?" On hearing these words the hair of their heads stood up and they could say nothing.

Then he plunged again into the waterfall and stood as before for two days, and on the second day eight boys appeared and grasped both his hands to draw him from the water, but he resisted them strongly and would not move. On the third day he again became as one dead, whereupon, that the waterfall should not be polluted, two heavenly youths, with their hair bound up tightly, descended from above the fall, and rubbed the whole body of Mongaku from head to foot with their warm and perfumed hands, so that he breathed again as one in a dream, and asked who it might be that thus had compassion on him.

"We are Kongara and Seitaka, the messengers of Fudo Myō-ō," replied the two youths, "and we have come in obedience to the command of the Myō-ō, 'Mongaku has made a sublime vow and is now under-

Mongaku under the waterfall.

going unparalleled austerites; go ye and succour him.'"

Then Mongaku cried with a loud voice; "Where is the abode of the Myō-ō?" "His abode is in the Tosotten, the fourth Heaven of Desire," they replied as they ascended far aloft above the clouds. Mongaku clasped his hands and exclaimed fervently: "Now am I full of hope, for even Fudo Myō-ō knows of my austerities;" and he again took up his position in the waterfall. But from henceforth he was favoured by most gracious signs of divine assistance; the bitter wind no longer pierced his body, and the falling water felt warm and soothing, and so he completed the three weeks of his vow and afterwards spent a thousand days in retirement at Nachi.

Then he started to travel round the whole country as a pilgrim, ascending Omine three times, Katsuragi twice, and then proceeding to Koya, Kogawa, Kinbusen, Hakusan, Tateyama, the peak of Fuji, Izu, Hakone, Togakushi in Shinano, and Haguro in Dewa, until at last, feeling a longing for his native province, he returned to the Capital, hardened like a well-tempered blade by his privations, and wise enough to pray down a flying bird from the sky.

THE CONTRIBUTION ROLL

Thereafter Mongaku retired to the mountain recesses of Takao to meditate. In this mountain was a temple called Shingoji, which Wake-no-Kiyomaro had built in the time of Shotoku Tenno, and which had not been repaired for a long time. In spring the mists filled it, and in autumn the fog was its only occupant; the doors had been blown down by the winds and lay rotting under the fallen leaves. The rain and dew had despoiled it of tiles, and the altar of Buddha stood bare to the sky. No priest abode there to read the Sutras, only the sun and moon shone betimes into it.

Mongaku, having made a vow to rebuild this temple, drew up a roll for donations and went round in all quarters to seek supporters, and in the course of his wanderings he came to the Hojuji-den where the Hō-ō was residing, and requested His Majesty to make a contribution. But it chanced that the Hō-ō was at the time engaged in some amusement and paid no attention, so Mongaku, who was naturally a bold and uncompromising character, knowing nothing of the Hō-ō's disinclination, but only thinking that the attendants had not told him, forced his way through into the Imperial Garden and shouted out loudly: "Oh most merciful Lord, how can it be that you pay no heed to such a matter as this?" And forthwith he spread out the roll and lifting it up high before him began to read:

"Contribution roll of the novice Mongaku, who, desiring to obtain the great blessedness of happiness in this world and in the world to come respectfully begs the assistance of all, high and low, priest and layman, in building a temple on the holy site of Mount Takao. When we consider it, all-embracing is the Eternal Mind. Though we use the appelations of Buddha and Mankind, albeit there is no distinction between these things, yet, since the clouds of Illusion accompanying the Buddha-nature spread thick over the mountain of

The intrusion of Mongaku.

the Twelve Causes of Existence, the Moon of the Pure Lotos of the mind is obscured and does not appear in the Great Abyss of the Three Poisons and Four Prides.

"Alas! how pitiable! The sun of Buddha quickly set, and dark and gloomy is the way of the revolving-wheel of births and deaths. So men give themselves up to passion and wine. Who will be grateful for the delusion of the raging elephant and the capering monkey? How can they who hate mankind and the Law hope to escape the torments of Emma and his jailers? I, Mongaku, though I have put away the dust of this world and donned the robe of the recluse, find evil Karma still mighty in my heart; day and night it arises, and the virtue that sprouts up within me becomes unpleasing to my ear and is cast away. Alas! how painful! Returning again to the fire-pits of the Three Ways, I must revolve through the grievous wheel of the Four Births, so that, through the ten thousand times ten thousand volumes of the Sakya Sage, revealing in every volume the affinity of the Buddha-seed, even the most true Law of Cause and Effect, it may not be impossible to attain to the Farther Shore of Perfect Enlightenment.

"Thus I, Mongaku, weeping at the gate of this life of impermanence, to encourage priests and laymen, high and low, to make connexion with the Paradise of the highest Lotus Throne, am intending to build a holy place for the Buddhas and Bodhisattvas. Takao-zan is a mount of high peaks, thick wooded like the Vulture Peak of Ghridrakuta, and of quiet valleys and mossy retreats like those of Shosando in China. The mountain streams gurgle and fall in foamy cascades, the apes scream in the crags and sport in the branches. Remote from the haunts of men, free from the dust and noise of the world, there is nothing to disturb our devotions: it is a very excellent site, most suitable for worshipping Buddha. The contributions are small; who is there who will not assist? Whoever gathers a little sand for a pagoda acquires merit in his Karma relation, how much more he who contributes even a small amount of money or property?

"So shall all both in city and country, far and near, rustics, priests, and laymen, sing of the Sovereign and this age and its contentment as the golden age of the rule of Yao and Shun in China, and smile as those who meet after a long parting. And if these sacred rites and mysteries are performed in their entirety, all shall attain to the Terrace of the True Gate of the One Buddha, and enjoy the immeasurable and innumerable blessings of the Three Buddha persons. The above composed by me Mongaku with the purpose of obtaining subscriptions as stated. The third month of the third year of Jisho."

The Exile of Mongaku

Now it happened that at this time the Prime Minister Myō-ōn-in was playing the lute and reciting, while Azechi-no-Dainagon Sukekata was playing the six-stringed Harp and his son Uma-no-kami Suketoki was singing and dancing the Saibara, Morisada, an attend-

The concert in the Hō-ō's Palace.

ant of the Fourth Rank, keeping time meanwhile and singing various Imayo measures, so that the Palace resounded with musical strains and they were all very merry.

The Hō-ō himself had deigned to join in the singing also, when suddenly the loud and strident voice of Mongaku broke in on their melody, spoiling the harmony and entirely upsetting the rhythm. "What is this?" exclaimed the Hō-ō in great wrath, "who is this boor who dares to interrupt Our Imperial Pleasure? Strike him down, some one!" At this the young and impetuous among the samurai in attendance rushed forward, each trying to be foremost, headed by one, Sukeyuki Hangwan by name, who shouted out, "Down with this villain who dares to disturb His Majesty's Amusement."

"I don't move from here until I receive the grant of a manor towards the cost of my temple on Mount Takao," replied Mongaku calmly, and then as he saw that they meant to attack him, shifting the roll to his other hand, he gave Sukeyuki Hangwan a blow on the head that knocked off his head-dress, and then doubling his fist struck him another in the chest that sent him flying backwards, so that he took to his heels and fled into the interior of the Palace.

He then drew from his bosom a dirk with the hilt wound with the hair of a horse's tail, and baring the blade stood waiting, ready to strike down any who approached. As he sprang round in all directions with the Contribution Roll in his left hand and the blade gleaming like ice in his right, it looked as if he had a sword in each hand. Nobles and Courtiers, terrified at such an amazing scene, ran about in all directions, so that the party of the Hō-ō was quite broken up and the whole Palace was in an uproar.

Then one of the Palace Guard, Ando Musha Migimune by name, drew his sword and rushed upon Mongaku, who also sprang forward to meet him. Ando Musha, not wishing to shed blood, turned the edge of his weapon and struck him a heavy blow with the back on his sword-arm, and then, as he staggered back a little, dropping his sword sprang on him with a shout to grapple with him. Mongaku, falling undermost, gripped his opponent's right arm as he did so and held on tight, but in spite of this Ando managed to seize him by the throat, and so, being about equal in strength, they rolled about in their struggles, now one being uppermost and now the other, until the others, who had held back so far, summoned up courage to rush in and overpower Mongaku and bind him, after which he was dragged out and handed over to the underlings of the constabulary. As they were taking him away, he drew himself up and glared at the Palace, crying out in a loud voice, the while he pranced up and down with anger: "So! not only do I get nothing, but I am treated in this outrageous manner. Know that the Three Worlds are to be consumed by fire, and how shall even the Palace of the Sovereign escape this fate? Even if one is an Emperor who boasts of the Ten Virtues, will he not descend to the Yellow Springs of Death and be tormented by the Ox-headed and Horse-headed Jailers of Hell?"

Then the order was given to put this insolent priest into prison and he was led off to be confined. Sukeyuki Hangwan, covered with shame at the ignominy of having his head-dress knocked off, did not appear at Court for a long time. Ando Musha, however, was rewarded for boldly seizing Mongaku by being at once promoted to the position of Uma-no-jo over the heads of others senior to him.

About this time it happened that the Empress Bifuku-mon-in died and there was a general amnesty so that Mongaku was set free, but as soon as he was let out he set forth again with his roll to collect contributions everywhere; and not only so, but wherever he went he proclaimed that the age was corrupt and that both the Emperor and his subjects would be destroyed, with the result that, as such disrespectful words could not be permitted, he was not allowed to remain in the Capital but banished to Izu.

Now Izu-no-kami Nakatsuna, the eldest son of Gensammi Nyūdō, was at this time Governor of Izu, and when this sentence was pronounced he gave orders that Mongaku should be brought to Izu by ship from the Tokaido, or Eastern Coast, and sent two or three inferior officials of the Kebiishi to take charge of him. These officers then said to him: "It is the custom for minor officials like ourselves to profit somewhat on these occasions; no doubt your reverence has many friends in various places, so when you are sent into exile to a far province, they will certainly wish to give you some presents, and food and necessaries for the journey; will you not then communicate with them?"

"I have few friends of that sort," replied Mongaku with a laugh, "but there is some one who lives on Higashi-yama who might perhaps do something for me; I will write a letter." Then they produced some very cheap paper, whereat Mongaku became very angry, exclaiming: "How do you expect me to write on paper like this;" and he threw it back at them. Then they got some good thick paper and handed it to him, but Mongaku laughed and said: "Unfortunately I cannot write, so please write the letter for me."

So one of them wrote at his dictation as follows: "I, Mongaku, having the intention of building a temple on Mount Takao, have been travelling about the country to raise money by subscription, but the age being such a one as it is, it has pleased the Emperor not only to refuse me any assistance, but even to banish me to the distant province of Izu. This being so I am much in need of supplies and comforts for the long journey, and beg that you will assist me in the matter." When he had written it, he asked to whom he should address it. "To the Goddess Kwannon at Kiyomizu," replied Mongaku. "Do you then make fools of minor officials like us?" they asked indignantly. "By no means," replied Mongaku, "I always rely on Kwannon of Kiyomizu in need, and indeed now I have no one else on whom to rely."

Then they took ship from the port of Ano in Ise, and when they came to Tenryu-nada in the province of

Tōtōmi a great tempest rose, and the ship seemed likely to be overturned by the mountainous waves. The helmsman and the sailors gave up all hope, and thinking their last hour had come, fell to praying, some calling on Kwannon and others repeating the Nembutsu of the dying.

Mongaku, however, was all this time lying asleep in the bottom of the ship, snoring loudly, until aroused by the confusion he suddenly sprang up, went to the side of the ship, and glaring angrily at the waves, shouted; "Ho! Thou Dragon King of the Waters! What meanest thou by endangering the ship in which is so holy a sage bound to accomplish a great vow. Knowest thou not, O most worthless of Dragon-Gods, that such conduct will receive the punishment of Heaven?" Then the wind and the waves were suddenly stilled and they arrived safely at the shores of Izu.

Now the trouble of the last few years, that is, the confinement of the Hō-ō in the Toba Palace the year before last, the execution of Prince Takakura the year after, and the troubled and critical state of the Empire generally, not to speak of the changing of the Capital, so wrought on the health of the Retired Emperor Takakura that he sickened and become very ill, and now, when he heard of the destruction of Tōdaiji and Kōfukuji, his condition grew serious, and at length on the fourteenth day of the same month he passed away at the Ikedono of Rokuhara, to the intense grief of the Hō-ō, after a reign of twelve years.

Autumn Leaves

While Takakura Tenno was on the Throne everybody declared that his consideration for others sur-
passed even that of the Mikados of the periods Enki
and Tenryaku, and though generally speaking it was
after he had attained to years of discrimination that he
obtained his reputation for wisdom and benevolence,
yet his disposition was kind and gentle from his earliest
childhood.

During the period Shoan, when His Majesty was
only about ten years old, being extremely fond of the
tinted leaves of autumn, he had a little hill-garden made
in the north enclosure of the Palace, and planted it
with maple and "haze" trees that redden beautifully in
that season, calling it "The Hill of Autumn Tints" and
from morning till evening he never seemed to tire of
looking at it.   But one night a late autumn gale blew
violently and scattered the leaves everywhere in confusion, so the next morning, when the Palace servants
went round early as usual to clean the grounds, they
swept up all the fallen leaves and the broken branches
as well, and as it was a bleak and cheerless morning
they made a fire with them in the court of the Nuidono,
and heated some *sake* to warm themselves.

Soon afterwards the Kurando in waiting, hastening
to inspect the garden before the Emperor should see it,
and finding nothing there, inquired the reason and the
servants told him.   "What?" he exclaimed, "how
could you dare to treat the garden that the Emperor is
so fond of in such a way? You deserve to be im-

The attendants of the Emperor Takakura warm their liquor.

prisoned or banished at least, and I too may very likely incur the Imperial displeasure." Just then the Emperor, coming out to see his favourite trees as soon as he had left his bed-chamber, was surprised to find they had all disappeared, and the Kurando told him what had happened. To his surprise His Majesty was not at all angry, but only laughed and quoted the Chinese poem by Po-chu-i about warming wine in the woods by burning maple-leaves. "I wonder" he said, "who can have taught it them. Really they are quite esthetes."

Again in the period Angen, one night when the Emperor was sleeping in a strange part of the Palace according to the advice of the diviners, being naturally wakeful, he could not get to sleep. Perchance it may be that, as the poem says, the voice of the Palace watchman makes a Monarch wakeful, or as the night was very cold he may have been thinking of the occasion when Saga Tenno, on just such a frosty night, feeling compassion for the suffering of his people, stripped off his own bed-clothes and exposed himself to the cold, and regretting that he himself could not emulate the virtue of such an Emperor. Thus being more wakeful than usual, he heard late at night the sound of some one crying out some distance away, and immediately summoned an attendant and ordered him to go and find out what it was.

When the Courtier on guard went out and searched, he discovered a poor girl in one of the lanes near carrying the lid of a clothes-chest and weeping bitterly. On his inquiring the cause, she told him that she was carrying home some clothes which her mistress, who was a lady-in-waiting at the Palace of the Hō-ō, could barely afford to have made, when two or three ruffians suddenly robbed her of them, and that her mistress could not continue to serve unless she had the proper clothes, and she did not know anyone who could help her, and so she was crying.

On hearing this the Courtier brought the girl back with him and reported the whole affair to the Emperor, who was moved to tears at the story. "Alas! how cruel," he exclaimed, "who could do such a thing? In the days of the Emperor Yao in China the people reflected the goodness of their Ruler and were good too, but now in this age the people have only me to imitate and so they are very wicked. When wrong is done in the Empire, ought I not to be ashamed?"

Then he asked what kind of garment it was, and on being told, he bade the Imperial Consort Kenrei-mon-in give her one of same kind, whereupon they brought a dress far more beautiful than the former one and gave it to the girl. Then the Emperor, fearful lest she might again be molested, as the hour was so late, ordered several of the Imperial Guards to escort her as far as the house of her mistress. It was not strange then that every one, even the poorest and meanest of his subjects, should pray for the long life of this virtuous Sovereign.

AOI-NO-MAE

Another story that has a certain pathetic interest is this. There was a certain little maiden who served one of the Empress's ladies-in-waiting, who was much beloved by the Emperor, and it was no ordinary passing fancy but a true and deep affection, so that her mistress no longer allowed her to wait on her, but rather treated her as her superior and paid her great deference and attention.

An ancient poem says: "Do not rejoice when a son is born, and do not despair when you have a daughter, for a son does not always become a Prince, while a daughter may become Imperial Consort and Empress." What a happy future might be before this little maid. She might become Nyōgō and Imperial Consort, then Mother of the Emperor and at last Retired Empress. Her name was Aoi-no-mae, but the ladies of the Court already spoke of her confidentially among themselves as Aoi-no-Nyōgō.

But when the Emperor heard of this he ceased to summon her to his presence: this was not because he had become tired of her, but because he feared the censure of the world, and being naturally of a brooding disposition he lost all taste for food, and falling sick became unable to leave the Imperial Bed-chamber.

Then the Regent Matsudono, hearing that His Majesty was thus depressed, hastened to the Palace to comfort him. "Why does Your Majesty thus fret about this affair?" he said, "for there is nothing to worry about. Let the maid be summoned again; her low rank need be no obstacle, for I will make her my adopted daughter and then she need fear no comparisons." "Ah no," replied the Emperor, "that cannot be; after I have retired from the Throne such a thing might be done, but the actions of a Reigning Emperor must be above the criticism of posterity."

So, as his Master would not at all entertain the idea, the Regent could do no more, but with tears in his eyes retired from the Palace. Afterwards the Emperor wrote this verse on a sheet of paper tinted in light green:

> Plain my love must be
> Though it is my earnest wish
> That it be not seen,
> For my friends come asking me
> Why I look so serious.

This was an old poem written by Taira Kanemori, but as it expressed his feelings the Emperor gave it to Reizei-no-Shonagon Takafusa to convey to Aoi-no-mae, who, when she had received it and read it, blushing deeply put it away in her bosom, and then, overcome by the violence of her feelings, immediately left the Court and returned to her home, where she took to her bed and died after about a week.

Kōgō

As the Emperor was so much grieved by this unhappy love episode the Empress sent one of her own ladies to him to console him. Her name was Kōgō and she was the daughter of Sakura-machi-no-Chunagon Shigenori, and not only was she the greatest beauty in the Palace but she was also without equal for her skill in playing the Koto. She had been beloved by Reizei-no-Dainagon Takafusa, and while he was only Shosho he sent her many poems and letters, but for some time they only accumulated without producing any effect, until at last she was moved to take pity on him and yielded. But now she was summoned to the side of the Emperor they could not but part, and for long her sleeves were moistened with tears of regret. The Shosho too was always going to the Palace to try if by any means he could see her once again, and used to loiter about in the neighbourhood of her apartment, but as she was now in the Emperor's household she would not exchange a word with him, or show, however indirectly, that she still had any tender feelings for him. Then the Shosho wrote a stanza and threw it so that it fell within the curtain of the room where she was. The lines ran as follows:

> I cannot bear it,
> For far as is the Northland
> She is removed.
> So far and yet so near—
> My love avails me nothing.

Though in her heart Kōgō would have liked to answer it, yet for the Emperor's sake and to avoid causing him any pain she did not even touch it, but bade one of her maids pick it up and throw it out into the courtyard. Takafusa could hardly contain his anger and disappointment at this treatment, but, remembering that if he were seen the results would be serious, he hastily picked up the paper, and, putting it in his bosom, returned to his house and gave vent to his feelings in these lines:

Alas! how cruel!
Even to touch my letter
She will not venture.
Yet how can I extinguish
The love that burneth in me?

And he prayed that he might die rather than continue
to live on in the world when he could no longer see her.

But when these things came to the ears of the Lay-
priest Chancellor he burst forth: "What a condition of
things is this! The Empress is my daughter and the
wife of Reizei Shosho is my daughter also, and how
does this Kōgō dare to take the husband of both? Let
her be put out of the way forthwith!"

Then Kōgō, caring nothing about her own fate, but
anxious lest the Emperor should in any way be
troubled, fled away one night from the Palace so that
no one knew whither she had gone. This grieved the
Emperor exceedingly, and he would not leave his bed-
chamber, but spent his days moping and in tears.
When Kiyomori heard of this he remarked: "Ah,
His Majesty is distressed about Kōgō I see, then something must be done," and he gave orders that none of
the Ladies-in-waiting were to be allowed to attend the
Emperor, and as he even frowned on other people who
paid visits, no one went to Court at all, since they did
not care to risk offending him, and all the Palace was
gloomy and deserted.

Now on the tenth day of the eighth month there was
a most beautiful moon without a trace of clouds in the
sky, and His Majesty was gazing at it, but as his eyes
were full of tears even the moon looked misty, and as
the hour grew late he called for one of his attendants,

but for some time no one answered, so deserted was the Palace. But a certain officer of the Palace Guard named Danjo-no-Daihitsu Nakakuni, who happened to be on duty that night, though in a remote part of the Palace, heard his master's voice through the silent halls and made reply.

Then the Emperor bade him come near, for he had something to ask, whereupon Nakakuni, wondering what it could be, entered the Imperial Chamber, and His Majesty inquired of him if he knew where Kōgō had hidden herself. "How should I know such a thing?" replied the retainer. "I have heard that she is living in a cottage with a single folding-door somewhere near Saga," said the Emperor, "but I do not know the name of the person with whom she is staying. Do you think you could find her?" "If I do not know the name of the master of the house, how can I find her?" replied Nakakuni in perplexity, whereat the Emperor in despair wept bitterly.

After some further thought Nakakuni remembered Kōgō's skill on the lute and said to himself: "Ah, on a moonlight night like this she will surely be thinking of His Majesty here in the lonely Palace, and no doubt she will play on the lute; now when she played in the Palace I used to be the one to accompany her on the flute, so none knows her playing as well as I, and if I go round about all the houses in the neighbourhood of Saga, why should I not find out where she is? Then" he said at last, "though I do not know in whose house she is lodging, I will go and search for her in that part, but if I find her and have no letter, perhaps I shall not be believed, so let Your Majesty write one that I may take it with me."

Then the Emperor gave him the letter and ordered him to take a horse from the Palace Stables, and he started off at a gallop, whipping up his horse under the clear light of the moon and singing as he rode the verse that begins: "The mountain village where the wild stag cries," feeling, no doubt, the pathos of the autumn scenery of Saga. So he rode on, stopping his horse to listen whenever he came to a cottage with a single folding-door, and wondering if the lady he sought was within, but no sound of a lute broke the silence. Then, wondering whether she had perhaps retired to some temple, he went to all the temples in that part, but still could find no trace of her. Then in a hamlet among the pines near Kameyama he thought he heard the sound of a lute; straining his ears he was uncertain whether it was not the blasts from the mountain-tops, or the soughing of the wind in the pine-trees. Urging on his horse he rode on farther and became aware that the sounds were indeed those of a lute, and that they proceeded from a cottage with a single folding-door, and stopping to listen awhile he perceived that without doubt the player was Kōgō, and that the piece she was playing was one called "Sōfūren," which expresses the longing felt by a wife for her absent husband.

Nakakuni was touched at the tender feeling for His Majesty that prompted her to select this piece from the many that she played, and drawing his flute from his girdle joined in the tune for a few bars, and then knocked softly at the door. The music immediately

ceased, whereupon Nakakuni called out: "It is Nakakuni who has come from the Palace with a message
from the Emperor;" but though he knocked several
times no one answered from within. After some time
there was a sound as of some one coming to the gate,
and as he stood there in joyful anticipation, the lock
was unfastened, and the gate opened a very little and
disclosed only the face of a beautiful young girl.

"Have you not mistaken the house?" she asked, "for
a Palace Messenger can have no errand here," whereat
Nakakuni, since he feared that if he made answer the
gate would be shut and locked again, pushed it open
by force and entered. Standing on the veranda of
the house he told his story: and he took out a letter and
handed it to her. The girl took it to Kōgō, who opened
and read it, and found that it was indeed His Majesty's
writing. In a short while she had written an answer
and sent it to Nakakuni with a lady's suit of Court
dress as a present. On receiving the answer he said:
"Although perhaps I ought not to ask for more than
this letter, yet as I was specially sent thither by my
Lord, and am not unknown to your mistress, how can I
return without a message from her own lips?"

Then Kōgō, consenting to his wish, came forth and
excused herself saying: "As you know, in fear of the
threatening and angry words of the Chancellor, I fled
away secretly one night from the Palace, and as I have
been staying in a place like this I have not played the
Koto at all but as I am going away to-morrow into the
recesses of Ohara, and this night is my last, the mistress
of this house persuaded me to play, saying that it was

late and there would be none to hear, and so I yielded, for the remembrance of former days stirred within me and my fingers yearned for my beloved instrument," and as she spoke her tears flowed freely, while Naka-kuni too hid his face in his sleeve.

After a while Nakakuni calmed his emotion and said: "Doubtless your intention in going into the recesses of Ohara is to become a nun; this, I think, is not a proper thing to do, for how will the Emperor feel about it? Nay, I can by no means allow it." and turning to his attendant he added; "See that this girl does not leave this place;" and leaving him there to guard the house, he sprung upon his horse and rode back again, reaching the Palace just as the dawn was beginning to break.

Tying up his horse and throwing the lady's dress over the Palace doors, he went toward the Shishinden, thinking that the Emperor would surely be sleeping by this time, and wondering who to send to him, but as it happened His Majesty was still sitting as he had left him the night before in melancholy abstraction, as the poet says:

Soaring up to the southward and wheeling round to the northward,
Vainly in autumn the goose seeks for the heat or the cold;
Flying forth to the eastward and sweeping round to the westward,
Ever its lonely eye stares at the moon of the dawn.

So Nakakuni came and gave him the letter of Kōgō and reported all he had done. The Emperor's joy was extreme, and he ordered him to go again that night and bring her back with him. Nakakuni, though he feared the wrath of Kiyomori if he should hear of it, yet as it was the Emperor's order, borrowed an ox-car from somebody and went down that night to Saga, and although Kōgō at first refused to accompany him, at last he prevailed on her and brought her back to the Palace.

There she lived secretly in a remote chamber, and used to visit His Majesty every night, so that in the course of time a Princess was born to her, and this is the Princess who is known as Bōmon-no-Nyōin. Then the matter came to the ears of the Lay-priest Chancellor and he was very angry, exclaiming: "Then it was all a lie that I was told that Kōgō had been got rid of; but at all events she shall be removed now," and somehow or other they decoyed her from the Palace and forced her to shave her head and become a nun. She was then only twenty-three years old, and though she had wished to retire from the world before, how sad a fate was it to be compelled to do so in this per-emptory manner, and to put on black robes and go and live in the wilds of Saga. It was these painful events that aggravated the illness of the Emperor so that he died. The Hō-ō had nothing but troubles, one coming fast after the other.

DEATH OF KIYOMORI

On the twenty-third day a Council of Courtiers was suddenly called at the Palace of the Hō-ō, the Sento Gosho, and Munemori addressed them thus: "The

The death of Kiyomori.

expedition we made into the East Country did not effect anything very much, so now I myself should like to take command and lead an army to chastize these rebels in the East and North." This bold speech was received with applause by all the rest, and they praised Munemori for his decisive action; the Hō-ō too seemed quite delighted, and every one who had the least experience of martial exercises, even though he might be a Courtier or Noble, declared himself ready to follow Munemori.

On the twenty-seventh day they intended to set out, but as Kiyomori had been taken ill during the night they did not move. On the twenty-eighth day is was reported that his condition was grave, and all Rokuhara and the Capital was in an uproar, every one running about and whispering together. From the day that the Chancellor was taken ill he could not drink even hot water, and the heat of his body was like a burning fire, so that if anyone came within eight or ten yards of him the heat was unbearable. All he could do was to mutter "Ata! Ata!" (Hot! Hot!): it was a most extraordinary sickness. To relieve him somewhat they brought water from the well of Senshuin on Hieizan and filled a stone tank with it, into which they lowered him, but the water began to bubble and boil and immediately became like a hot bath.

When water was poured on him from a pipe, it flew off again hissing in clouds of steam and spray, as though it had struck red-hot iron or stone, and the water that did strike him burst into flames so that the whole chamber was filled with whirling fires and thick black smoke. It must have been just such a sight that Hōgyō Sōzu saw formerly when he entreated Emma, the King of Hades, to show him the place where his mother was; for Emma, moved by his prayers, sent his jailers to guide him to the hottest Hell, and when he had passed through the iron gate he saw the flames shooting up like meteors, thousands of miles high.

Moreover the wife of the Chancellor, Hachijo-no-Nii-dono, had a terrible dream. She dreamed that a flaming chariot entered the gate of her mansion without any driver, and in front and behind it stood two creatures, one with the head of an ox and the other with that of a horse, while on the front of the chariot appeared an iron tablet inscribed with the single character MU, signifying Not. The Nii Dono, in her dream, asked whither it had come, and the answer was: "Because the evil Karma of the Priestly Chancellor of the Heike is so great, this chariot has come to fetch him from the Palace of Emma-Ō the Dread King." "Then," said she, "what is the meaning of that tablet?" "Because of the crime of the burning of the great bronze image of Vairochana a hundred and sixty feet high, it has been decreed at the tribunal of Emma-Ō that he shall go down to the Avichi Hell, the hottest of the hot hells where rebirth is unceasing, and so it is that the character Not has been written; but the character signifying 'Cease' has not yet been written."

Then the Nii Dono awoke, bathed in a cold sweat; and when she told what she had seen, the hair of all that heard it stood up with affright. Then they hastened to offer gold and silver and all manner of precious things to the shrines and temples of the gods and Buddhas, and fetched thither their horses and saddles and armour and swords and bows and arrows, and prayed with might and main, but no sign was vouch-safed them; and the Courtiers and their wives assembled around the bed of the Nyūdō and mourned and lamented bitterly.

On the second day of the second month, this year being leap-year, the Nii Dono came to the bedside of the Chancellor, in spite of the intensity of the heat, and said: "Though my visits to inquire about you every day may seem few, yet perchance, while still you are able, you may tell me of something that you desire." Then Kiyomori, though his sufferings were so great, summoned up his fast-failing strength and said in a weak voice:

"Since the time of Hogen and Heiji my unworthy house subdued the enemies of the Emperor many times and thereby gained great rewards, for which we are most grateful, and I, having been permitted to become the maternal relation of the Heavenly Sovereign and to reach the office of Prime Minister am about to hand down my glory to my descendants, wherefore in this world I have nothing else left to desire. The only thing I have to regret is that I cannot see the head of Yoritomo. When I am dead do not perform any Buddhist services or make offerings for me, or build temples or pagodas; only make haste and slay Yori-tomo and cut off his head and lay it before my tomb. That will be the best offering you can make me either in this world or the next."

So deep indeed was his guilt. Then they put water on a board and rolled him on it to ease him, but it did no good, and on the fourth day of the same month he at last expired in great anguish. When it was known the commotion and galloping to and fro of horses and carriages was such as to make the sky echo and the earth tremble. Even if he had been the Heavenly Sovereign, the Lord of ten thousand chariots, it could hardly have been greater.

He was sixty-four years old this year. He cannot be said to have died of old age, for when the result of man's karma comes upon him the most potent Sutras have no efficacy, nor can the power of the gods and Buddhas avail anything; yea, all the deities of heaven cannot protect him, so what can ordinary men do? Even if tens of thousands of loyal warriors, all willing to lay down their lives for him, were ranged around both above and below, they could not fight with the unseen and invulnerable powers of the underworld. And so alone and without a companion he must go down to the Yellow Springs of Death, across the Sanzu-no-kawa, the river of Hades, and ascend the Mountain of Shide whence no traveller returns. And the evil karma that he has made will take shape as the jailers that come to meet him.

And so, as it must be, on the seventh day his funeral pyre was lighted at Otaki, and Enjitsu Hogen took his bones and brought them down to the province of Settsu, where they were desposited at Kyogashima. Thus though he wielded such great authority that his name was feared through the whole Empire, his body rose up in smoke to the sky of Kyoto, and his bones mingled with the sand of the shore.

THE ADVENTURES OF THE PRIEST JISHIN

It was said, as has been related, that Kiyomori was not an ordinary man at all, and it was rumoured that he was an incarnation of Jie Sojo.* The reason for this was the following story. In the temple of Seichoji in the province of Settsu there lived a certain saintly monk named Jishin Bo Sonei. He had formerly been attached to Hieizan, where for many years he had meditated on the Hokke Sutra, but at last his religious zeal drove him to leave that mountain and come and live in this temple, so that all believed in him and were converted.

On the twenty-second day of the twelfth month of the period Shoan, Sonei went as usual to the altar of Buddha to perform the evening service, and was sitting supported by his arm-rest reading the Lotus Sutra, when, it seemed neither in a dream or reality, there entered two men clad in white Kariginu and Eboshi and wearing leggings and straw sandals, carrying an open letter. When Sonei, as in a dream, asked them from whom they had brought it, they replied: "From the Court of Emma-Ō," whereupon he received it from their hands and opening it read as follows:

"To the Priest Jishin Bo Sonei, residing in the temple of Seichoji, in the province of Settsu, in the

---

*A famous priest who became Tendai Zasshu. Died in the third year of Ei-kwan (985). Also called Ryogen.

Country of Dai-Nihon which is in the Djambudvipa.
On the twenty-sixth day at the Palace of Emma
there will be held a recitation of the ten myriad por-
tions of the Hokke Sutra, and ten myriad priests from
ten myriad countries will be entertained. As you have
been included in the number do you proceed hither as
appointed. The above given at his Court, at the command of Emma-Ō. Twenty-second day of the twelfth
month of the second year of Shoan."

As Sonei could by no means refuse the dread command, he wrote an acknowledgment, after which he
awoke, and when he related the vision to Ko-ei, the
chief priest of the temple, the hair of all who heard it
stood up with affright. Thinking that his end was
near he gave himself up to prayer, repeating the Nembutsu continually, and trusting that Buddha would have
compassion on him and receive him into his Paradise.
On the twenty-fifth day he went as usual to the altar
of Buddha and recited the Sutras, and at the hour of
the Rat (12 p.m.), feeling sleepy, he returned to his
room and lay down to rest.

As the hour of the Ox, (2 a.m.) the two men came
again and urged him to start with them, but when
Sonei was preparing to go, he found that he had no
proper garments or begging-bowl. While he was
wondering what was to be done, for it would be a
dreadful thing to disobey the mandate of Emma-Ō, a
priest's robe suddenly wrapped itself round his body,
while a begging-bowl of gold descended from heaven
into his hand; at the same time two attendant-priests,
two acolytes and ten lower priests appeared before his

apartment with a chariot adorned with the seven precious things. Sonei joyfully mounted the chariot, which soared away through the sky toward the northwest and soon reached the Palace of Emma. Around it spread on all sides an immense courtyard, and the vastness of its spaces within was indescribable.

The Palace buildings were all of gold and jewels, and shone with a brightness scarcely to be borne by mortal eyes. The service of that day had already been finished and the priests had all departed, so Sonei stood waiting in the middle gate on the south side of the Palace, viewing the buildings from far off.

While he stood thus, all the officials and attendants of Emma's realm came to make their obeisance to the Dread King in a procession of extraordinary magnificence, and Sonei, wishing to inquire about his sins and his future life, proceeded in the same direction. As he did so the ten attendants formed into line and the two priests carried boxes, while the acolytes held an umbrella over him, and in this way they approached the presence of Emma; whereupon the King and all his officials and Courtiers rose up to greet them, for the two priests now appeared in their real form as Yakuo Bosatsu and Yusei Bosatsu, and the two acolytes as Tamonten and Jikokuten, the ten attendants being metamorphosed into ten female demons who ministered to him.

"Why have you come thus when all the other priests have departed?" asked Emma. "From my childhood," replied Sonei, "I have never neglected daily to recite the Hokke Sutra, but even so I am not sure of my

The priest Jishin Sonei in the presence of Emma-ŏ,
King of Hades.

fate in the after life, so it is of that that I wish to inquire." "Rebirth in Paradise," answered Emma, "is granted according to faith, but the Hokke Sutra is the straight way for man to attain Buddhahood, for which purpose all the Buddhas of the Three Worlds appeared on this earth. The merit of earnest faith and understanding of it is greater than that of practise of the Five Paramitas, while the virtue of preaching it five times is more potent than eighty years charity. According to your abounding merit you will be reborn into the highest circle of the Tuchita heaven."

Then, turning to an attendant, the Dread King said: "The deeds of this man's life are in the casket of good works; go and fetch them, and show him what is written." Then the ministering demon went to the storehouse on the south side and brought the casket, and when he opened it and read what was written therein, every act and every thought that he had done or meditated in his whole life was revealed; not one was lacking. "One request only I have to make," said Sonei, bursting into tears, "show me, I beseech thee, the way by which I may escape from the endless circle of births and deaths, and attain to the highest state of Enlightenment." So, as he ceased not from his tears, Emma, moved by compassion, instructed him in these sacred words of doctrine:

> Wife and child and kindred, rank and wealth,
> Accompany no mortal after death,
> But devils formed from the ill deeds he did,
> Torment him that he scream for evermore.

Sonei was exceedingly rejoiced and said: "In the country of Dai-Nihon in the Djambudvipa, at Wadamisaki in the province of Settsu, the Lord High Chancellor of the Heike has built cells extending over a distance of ten cho square, and invited many priests to come and recite the Sutras and pray earnestly, even as it might be at the meeting of to-day." On hearing this, Emma in great admiration and gladness exclaimed: "That Nyūdō is no ordinary person; he is the reincarnation of Jie Sojo, and it was because he kept the law of Tendai Buddhism that for a while he was born again in Japan. Three times a day we pray for him here in these words which you will remember to repeat to the Nyūdō.

> Jie Dai-Sojo greatly we revere,
> Protector of the Tendai Buddhist Law.
> Revealed on earth as the Great Chancellor,
> His evil Karma even will help mankind.

So, being entrusted with these holy words, Sonei went out from the presence of the King of the Underworld, weeping tears of joy, and when he came to the middle gate of the south side, his ten priestly attendants again brought the chariot and soared away with him toward the south-west, so that he seemed to have returned in the twinkling of an eye, whereupon he awoke as from a dream. Afterwards, going up to Kyoto, he went to the mansion of the Nyūdō at Nishihachijo and told him all that he had seen.

Kiyomori was greatly rejoiced, and after entertaining him royally, sent him away with many presents, beside raising him to the rank of Risshi. And this is how it came to pass that all knew that the Nyūdō was the reincarnation of Jie Sojo. Jikyo Shonin was also the reincarnation of Kobo Daishi, while the Retired Emperor Shirakawa was the reincarnation of Jikyo Shonin. This Emperor accumulated many meritorious actions and piled up many virtuous deeds, and in this degenerate age also Kiyomori, as the reincarnation of Jie Sojo, both by his evil deeds and his virtuous actions acquired great merit, and thus conferred much benefit on himself and mankind. Not otherwise was it that S'akya Muni and Devadatta both greatly helped the world of men.

Now when Kiso Yoshinaka had coerced the districts of the east and north, he was ready to make an attack on Kyoto, and as the Heike had announced during the winter of the previous year that they would probably move in the spring, the levies from the Sanin, Sanyo, Nankai and Saikai districts came pouring in like mist and clouds. As for the Tosan or Eastern Hill district, the men of Ōmi, Mino and Hida came in, but on the Tokaido none joined them from eastward of Ōmi. All the western districts sent their men, but from the Hokurikudo not one arrived from north of Wakasa. After a Council of Courtiers had been held, the Heike leaders decided to proceed against Kiso Yoshinaka first, and then to attack Yoritomo, and with this purpose their army set out for the north. The Commanders-in-Chief were Komatsu-no-Sammi Chūjō Koremori and Echizen-no-Sammi Michimori, while the Vice-Commanders were Satsuma-no-kami Tadanori, Kōgō-gū no-suke Tsunemasa, Awaji-no-kami Kiyofusa and Mikawa-no-kami Tomonori. Six generals were appointed to lead the samurai, Etchū-no-Jirōhyōye Moritsugu, Kazusa-no-taiyu Hangwan Tadatsuna, Hida-no-taiyu Hangwan Kagetaka, Kawachi-no-Hangwan Hidekuni, Takahashi-no-Hangwan Nagatsuna and Musashi-no-Saburosaemon Arikuni, beside whom there were three hundred and forty other valiant warriors apt to command. The forces under them were about a hundred thousand horsemen, and at the hour of the Dragon (8 a.m.) on the seventeenth day of the fourth month they left Kyoto for the north country. As their supplies were insufficient, as soon as they had crossed the pass of Ausaka outside the Capital, they began to seize and appropriate anything they wanted from the estates and houses that lay by the way, not sparing even the government property. As they went along by Shiga, Karasaki, Mikawajiri, Mano, Takashima, Shiozu and Kaizu, the inhabitants of these places could not endure it and fled to the mountains.

CHIKUBUSHIMA

Now the Generals Koremori and Michimori pressed on their way, but Tadanori, Tsunemasa, Kiyofusa and Tomonori tarried a while at Shiozu and Kaizu in Omi. Of these Kōgō-gū-no-suke Tsunemasa had excelled in poetry and music from his youth up, and it happened that one morning, wishing to calm his mind in the midst of these alarms and disorders, he went out to the edge of the lake to enjoy the scenery. As he looked out into the offing he saw an island in the distance, and calling to Tōhyōye-no-Jō Arinori who had accompanied him, he asked what island it was.

"That is the famous island called Chikubushima;" replied Arinori, whereupon Tsunemasa expressed a wish to go out to it, so they got a small boat and escorted by Arinori and Anemon-no-Jo Morinori with six retainers, he crossed over to Chikubushima. It was the eighteenth day of the fourth month, but still the song of the bush-warbler of the vale lingered among the green twigs and recalled the favours of spring, and the ever charming early notes of the cuckoo answered it, while the clusters of wistaria hung heavy on the pines. The scene filled Tsunemasa with ecstasy, and he quickly alighted from the boat and climbed up on to the island, gazing at the beauty of the landscape with a heart too full for words. Not fairer it seemed was that magic island of Horai, whither Shi Huang of Ts'in sent many fair youths and maidens, and Wu Ti of Han dispatched a magician, if haply they might find it and bring back from thence the water of youth and immortality, but not finding it, and fearing to return to China, age overtook them in their ships while they were still vainly searching the boundless ocean. And in one of the Sutras it is written: "In the Djambud-vipa is a certain lake; and in the midst of it, proceeding from the bottom of the world, there is an isle, formed all of crystal, where fairy maidens dwell." And this, they say, is the island.

Then Tsunemasa, respectfully approaching the Myōjin, the deity of the place, prayed thus: "O thou goddess Benzaiten, who wert known of old under the title of Nyorai, and doest deign to manifest thyself here in a spiritual body as a saviour; for though we may

Tsunemasa plays before the shrine.

address thee by the names of Myo-on-ten and Benzai-ten, yet in this place thou art united in one body to save mankind; grant, we beseech thee, the petitions and desires that we offer before thee."

And as he was still kneeling before the shrine the dusk fell over the lake, and the waiting moon rose over the water so that it turned into silver, and the white beams bathed the steps of the shrine with light. Then the priest who lived there, knowing Tsunemasa's skill in music, brought him a Biwa, and he played and sang the melodies called Jōgen and Sekijo, so that the liquid notes rang clear through the silent shrine. So exquisite it was that the Myōjin could not restrain her emotion, but appeared over the shoulder of Tsunemasa as he played, in the form of a white dragon. Tsunemasa, overcome by reverential awe, laid aside his Biwa and composed the stanza:

> Lo! the deity
> Of the dread swift-flashing blade
> Deigns to show herself.
> May it be a blessed sign
> That my humble prayer is heard.

And so, not doubting that the enemies of the Throne would soon be subdued and the insurgents put to flight, he embarked in the boat and returned to the mainland in great joy.

SHINOHARA

Now the Heike had retreated to Shinohara in the province of Kaga to gain time to rest their men and horses, but Kiso Yoshinaka pursued after them with fifty thousand horsemen, and on the twentieth day of

the fifth month he again confronted them. Imai Shirō
Kanehira immediately rode forward with five hundred
men, and against him from the Heike ranks came
Hatakeyama Shōji Shigeyoshi, Oyamada-no-Bettō
Arishige and Utsunomiya-no-Saemon Tomotsuna with
three hundred. These knights were often in Kyoto
on guard duty, and as they were veteran warriors
Munemori had sent them to the North Provinces to
assist in the campaign with their advice.

So Hatakeyama and Imai detached first five, and then
ten of their samurai to begin the contest and see who
would prove the better, after which the two forces
attacked each other in mingled combat. It was
at high noon on the twenty-first day that they joined
battle, and both sides fought fiercely and stubbornly,
while the sun shone hot over their heads and there was
no breeze even to move a blade of grass, so that the
sweat poured down over their bodies as if they had
been plunged in water.

At last, when most of his retainers had fallen,
Hatakeyama was compelled to retire, though on Imai's
side also very many men were slain. Then Takahashi-
no-Hangwan Nagatsuna with five hundred men came
forth from the Heike, and Higuchi-no-Jirō Kanemitsu
and Ochiai-no-Gorō Kaneyuki with three hundred rode
out from Kiso's force to meet them, and for some time
both parties fought on the defensive; Takahashi's
men, however, being samurai from various provinces,
did not stand the onset, but broke and fled, each for
himself, heedless of the orders of their leader. Takahashi himself, though a most valiant fighter, was forced

to retreat for lack of support, and rode away alone to the southward.

Then Nyūzen-no-Kotarō Yukishige of Etchū, burning to overcome so stout an adversary, urged on his horse with whip and stirrup and overtook him. Coming up beside him he closed and grappled with him, but Takahashi gripped him hard, and pinned him against the front of his saddle so that he could not move, crying at the same time: "Who are you, sir! Declare your name and titles!" "I am Nyūzen-no-Kotarō Yukishige of the Province of Etchū, and my age is eighteen!" replied his assailant. On hearing this the tears ran down Takahashi's face as he exclaimed: "Ah, how pitiful! If my lad, who fell last year, had lived till now, he would be just eighteen; I ought to twist your neck and cut off your head, but as it is I will let you go:" and he released him.

Then Takahashi got off his horse to recover his breath and wait to see if any of his retainers would come up, and Nyūzen also dismounted, but, still thinking what a feat it would be to kill such a famous leader, even though he had just spared his life, he cast about to see how he could take him unawares. Takahashi, never dreaming of such treachery, was talking to him quite without reserve, when Nyūzen, who was famed for the rapidity of his movements, catching him off his guard, suddenly drew his sword and aimed a lightning thrust under his helmet. Just then, as he staggered back from the blow, three of Nyūzen's retainers came up, and Takahashi, stout warrior though he was, was borne down by superior numbers and slain.

The Death of Sanemori

Now among the retreating Heike retainers was Nagaino-Saitō Bettō Sanemori of Musashi, and he had a certain intention in his mind. He was clad in a red brocaded hitatare over armour with green lacing, and on his head was a helmet surmounted by lofty horns. He wore a gold-mounted sword and a quiver of twenty-four arrows with black and white feathers, and his bow was of black lacquer bound with red rattan. He rode a grey horse with black spots and his saddle was richly ornamented with gold. Though his companions kept on retiring, he alone continued to turn back and engage the enemy to protect their rear.

Then one of Kiso's men named Tezuka-no-Tarō rode forward and shouted to him; "How splendid! Though all your side are in flight, you only, one single knight, dare to face us alone in such gallant fashion; I pray you declare your name." "Who then are you that ask?" replied Sanemori. "I am Tezuka-no-Tarō Kanesashi-no-Mitsumori of Shinano," answered the other. "Then," replied Sanemori, "you will suit me well; and I too shall not disgrace your arms, though, for a certain reason I cannot declare my name. Come on Tezuka! A grapple!"

But as he rushed upon him, one of Tezuka's retainers, fearful that his master might be slain, thrust himself in between and received the onslaught. "Ho! who are you that wishes for the honour of being sped by the greatest warrior in Nippon?" cried Sanemori, as he caught him in his arms and pressed him tight against the front of his saddle so that he could not move, the while he twisted his neck round and cut off his head.

Tezuka himself, seeing his retainer thus fall, slipped round to the left side of his opponent, and lifting the skirts of his armour, stabbed him twice and then pulled him from his horse, weakened as he was from the wounds. Thus, spite of his great strength and valour, fell Saitō Sanemori, for he was wearied with his long struggle, besides being well advanced in years.

Then Tezuka, giving the head to one of his men who ran up, came into the presence of Kiso Yoshinaka and bowed low. "I have brought your lordship," said he, "the head of a strange fellow whom I have fought with and slain. He might be a great leader, but he had no following; he might be a simple samurai, but he wears a hitatare of brocade. When I bade him declare his rank, he demanded mine but would not give his own. His speech is that of one of the warriors of the Eastland."

"Ah," exclaimed Yoshinaka, "this must be Saitō Bettō. Indeed? I remember seeing him once when I went over to Kōzuke; I was only a small boy then but I think his hair was nearly white, so he must be over seventy now, and ought to be quite white-haired; but this hair and beard is black. Ho, there! summon Higuchi-no-Jirō Kanemitsu; he is about the same age as Sanemori and knew him well." Higuchi, answering the summons, entered, and after a single glance at the head, burst into tears: "Alas!" he exclaimed, "it is indeed Saitō Bettō." "Then," said Yoshinaka, "how is it that his hair is still black, for he must be more than seventy?"

Higuchi, repressing his tears, replied: "Ah, that the pitifulness of his fate should have moved me to these weak tears; still, we warriors are apt to be touched by the recollection of even these trifling things. I remember when we were talking together, as we were often wont to do, that he said to me; 'I am over sixty now, but if I go to fight again I shall dye my hair black and become young once more, for I will not be pitied as a decrepit old knight, or look foolish if I strive for place among the youthful blades.' Verily his hair is only dyed, and if you have it washed my words may be proved." So Kiso ordered the head to be washed forthwith, and the hair turned white even as Higuchi had said.

With regard to Sanemori's wearing a hitatare of brocade the reason was this. When he went to take leave of the Daijin Munemori he said to him: "There is one request that I wish to make, and it concerns me alone. Last year, when I went down with our men to the Eastern Provinces, I was startled by the noise of the water-fowl and fled in panic from Kambara in Suruga without so much as shooting one arrow, and that was a disgrace to my old age. Now I am going on the campaign in the North and there I intend to die. It was in that land that I was born, in Echizen, and it is only of late years that I have lived in Nagai of Musashi, the domain that your bounty has bestowed upon me. According to the proverb: 'Wear brocade when you return to your birth place,' I beg your lordship, if it is not too much to ask, to allow me the favour of wearing a hitatare of brocade." Munemori, touched by the gallantry of his address, gave him permission forthwith. As in China Chu Mai Ch'en flaunted his brocaded sleeves at Hui Chi Shan so Saitō Bettō Sanemori would make a name in the North Country. Imperishable, though vain, is the reputation he made, while his corpse mingles with the dust of the Northland. Thus of the ten thousand men of the Heike who set out from the Capital on the seventeenth day of the fourth month, ready to confront any foe, barely twenty thousand returned at the end of the fifth. "If you fish out all the rivers, you will get a lot of fish, but next year there will be none; if you burn the cover to hunt you will catch a lot of beasts, but next year there will be none; it would have been wiser to have taken thought for the future and kept some behind," was the opinion of most people.

DEPARTURE OF THE EMPEROR FROM THE CAPITAL

As the Chinese poet says: "The Imperial Capital is a place ever busy with fame and gain; after cockcrow it has no rest." If this is so when it is quietly governed, what must it be when all is confusion. Doubtless they would have liked to flee to the innermost recesses of Mount Yoshino, but their enemies were in possession of all the highroads and all the provinces were hostile, so that they could only find refuge by the sea. As we read in the golden words of the Hokke Sutra; "In the Three Worlds there is no rest; it is even as a house

that has taken fire." Not otherwise was the state of
the Capital at this time. On the twenty-fourth day at
dusk Munemori went to the Ikedono at Rokuhara
where the Empress Kenrei-mon-in was staying and
said: "Kiso Yoshinaka is coming up to attack the
Capital with fifty thousand horsemen, and has already
arrived in Higashi-Sakamoto in Ōmi, where the monks
of Hieizan have joined him; we must stay here at all
events, but as it would be most unfortunate if either
yourself or your august mother the Nii Dono came to
any harm, we think it best that you, with the Emperor
and the Hō-ō, should for a while retire to the Western
Provinces." "As affairs now are," replied the
Empress, "that will be perhaps the best plan;" and as
she spoke her feelings overcame her and she sobbed
unrestrainedly into the sleeve of her Imperial Robe.
Munemori also moistened the sleeve of his garment
with his tears.

Now when the Hō-ō heard privately of this design
of the Heike to take him away to the Western Provinces, he departed secretly from his Palace at midnight, attended only by Uma-no-kami Suketoki, and
made an Imperial Progress by himself to some place
the whereabouts of which remained augustly unknown.
And no one was aware of it.

When it was known that the Hō-ō was no longer in
the city the excitement was extraordinary, and the
flurry and confusion of the Heike was such that it
seemed that it could have hardly been greater if the
enemy had actually been entering the houses of the
Capital. As they had thus made preparations to send

the Emperor and the Hō-ō to the Western Provinces
and then found that their plan was already upset, they
felt like one who takes refuge under a tree that does
not keep off the rain.   However they determined to
carry out their design in the case of the Emperor at
least, so at the hour of the Hare (6 a.m.) the Imperial
Palanquin was made ready, His Majesty being at this
time a child of six years old, and knowing nothing of
what was taking place.

His Imperial Mother Kenrei-mon-in rode also in the
same Palanquin.   Hei-Dainagon Tokitada-no-Kyō had
given orders that all the Treasures of the Imperial
House should be taken with them, the Sacred Jewel,
the Sword, the Mirror, the Imperial Seal and Key, the
Tablet for marking the hours, and the Imperial Biwa
and Koto, but such was the flurry and excitement that
many of them were left behind.   His Majesty's own
sword was also forgotten in the hurry.   Tokitada-no-
Kyō and his two sons Kura-no-kami Nobumoto and
Sanuki-no-Chūjō Tokizane accompanied the procession
in full court robes, while the Imperial Guard of the
Konoe-tsukasa and the Mitsuna-no-suke escorted them
in armour, carrying their bows and quivers.   So they
proceeded along the Shichijō to the west and the Shujaku to the south.

When the Heike fled from the Capital they set fire
to all their mansions, and Rokuhara, Ikedono, Komat-
sudono, Hachijō Nishi-hachijō and others, in all
twenty mansions, beside some forty or fifty thousand
houses of their retainers in the city and in Shirakawa,
went up in flames.

Thus the places that the Emperor used to frequent were reduced to ashes, and nought but the foundation-stones was left of his residences; the Imperial Car was his only refuge. Of the gardens of the Princesses but the site remains, and on the place of their elegant chambers the dew falls like tears and the blasts whine mournfully. The splendid apartments where the ladies tired themselves behind the long curtains, the hunting-lodges and fishing-pavilions, the residence of the Regent, the mansions of the Courtiers, the labour of many years made vain in an hour, what now remained of them but charred logs? How much more the lodgings of their retainers and the houses of the common people? In all the area that the fire devoured was a score of cho and more. Not otherwise, when the power of Wu was overthrown, the terraces of Ku Su were suddenly abandoned to the thistles and dew, and when the might of Ts'in was at last laid low, the smoke of the palace of Hien Yang obscured the land. Though the slopes of the pass of Han Ku were made strong, the northern barbarians broke through, and though they relied on the deep waters of the Yellow River the eastern marauders took possession of it.

DEPARTURE OF TADANORI FROM KYOTO

Satsuma-no-kami Tadanori, who had already left the Capital, wishing to see Gojō-no-sammi Shunsei once again, rode back again to the city with a small train of five retainers and a page, all, like himself, in full armour. When he came to the gate of the mansion, however, he found it shut fast, and even when he called his name, it was not opened, though there was a sound of people running about within crying out that one of the fugitives had returned.

Then Satsuma-no-kami hastily dismounted from his horse and himself cried out with a loud voice: "It is I, Tadanori, who have come; I have something to say to Sammi-dono; if you will not open the gate, at least beg him to come forth here that I may speak with him." "If it is indeed Tadanori," replied Shunsei, "you need have no fear, but admit him." Then they opened the gate and he entered, and the meeting between the two was most moving and pathetic. "Ever since I became your pupil in the art of poetry years ago," said Tadanori, "I have never forgotten you, but for the last few years the disorder of the Capital and the risings in the provinces have prevented me from coming to see you.

"Now the final scene in the fall of our house hurries on apace, and the Emperor has already departed from the Capital. But there is one thing that I very greatly desire. Some time ago I heard that an Anthology of Poems was to be made by the Imperial Command, and I wished to ask if you would condescend to submit one of my poor verses for consideration, that my name may be remembered in time to come; and I felt great regret when the Collection was postponed owing to the unsettled state of the country. If, however, at some time in the future, when peace is restored to the Empire, this Anthology should be made, I would beg your favour for one of the stanzas in this scroll, that my spirit may rejoice under the shade of the long grass, and from that far-off world may come and aid you."

And with these words he drew out from beneath the sleeve of his armour a scroll containing a hundred verses that he considered to be the best he had so far composed and handed them to Shunsei. "Truly does this memento show that you have not forgotten me," replied Shunsei as he opened and perused it, "and I find it hard to keep back my tears when I think of the manner of your coming. Verily the sadness of it is unutterable and your affection to me most deep."

"Whether my bones will bleach on the hills or my name be echoed by the billows of the Western Sea, I care not," answered Tadanori, "for I feel no regret for this fleeting world; and so, as it must be, farewell;" and he sprang upon his horse, and, replacing his helmet on his head, rode away to the westward. Sammi-dono stood looking after him a long while until he was out of sight, and as he looked the words of the following Chinese verse were borne back to his ears in the voice, as it seemed, of Tadanori:

> Far is the road I must travel; so do I gallop
> into the evening mists of Yen Shan.

Overcome by his melancholy thoughts, Shunsei controlled his feelings with difficulty as he slowly returned to his mansion.

In after days, when the Empire was once more at peace, an Imperial Order was issued to make an Anthology called the Senzai-shū, and Shunsei remembered the request of Tadanori and his conversation, but though there were many verses worthy of immortality in the scroll that he had written, as at that time he and all the Heike had been declared to be rebels against the Throne, all that he could do for the memory of his unhappy disciple was to include one of them under the title of "A flower of my native land," by "An unknown author." The stanza runs thus:

> See the rippling waves
> Lapping ever Ōmi's strand
> Where once Shiga stood.
> 'Tis no more, but on the hills
> Still the mountain cherry blooms.

DEPARTURE OF TSUNEMASA FROM KYOTO

Kōgō-gū-no-suke Tsunemasa, the eldest son of Shūri-no-taiyū Tsunemori, had, as a child, served as page to the Imperial Abbot of the temple of Omuro Ninnaji, and still felt so deeply attached to him that he determined to pay him a farewell visit, even in spite of their great haste; so he took five or six retainers with him, and, riding off thither at great speed, hurriedly alighted from his horse and knocked at the gate.

"Our Sovereign has already departed from the Capital," he said, "and the doom of our house is at hand but all I regret in this fleeting world is that I must part from my lord. Since I first entered this Palace cloister at the age of eight until my Gempuku at the age of thirteen, except for a slight interval of sickness, never did I leave my lord's side; but to-day, alas, I must go forth to the wild waves of the Western Sea, not knowing when, if ever, I shall return. So I have come, wishing to see his face more, though I feel ashamed to enter his presence in this rough soldier's garb."

When he heard this, the Imperial Abbot, moved with compassion, replied: "Bid him enter as he is, without changing his dress." Tsunemasa was that day attired in a hitatare of purple brocade and body armour laced with green silk. A gold-mounted sword hung at his side and a quiver of twenty-four arrows with black and white feathers at his back, and under his arm he carried his bow of black lacquer with red binding. Taking off his helmet and hanging it from his shoulder, he reverently entered the little garden before the apartment of the Abbot. His Reverence immediately appeared and bade them raise the curtain before the veranda, on which he invited Tsunemasa to be seated.

When Tsunemasa had seated himself he beckoned to Tōhyōye-no-Jō Arimori who attended on him, and he brought a bag of red brocade containing his master's lute, which Tsunemasa laid before the Abbot. "I have brought back this famous Biwa 'Seizan,' which Your Reverence presented to me last year, with deep regret, for it is not proper that I should take such a thing, one of the most precious treasures of our land, into the rude wilds of the country. May I then deposit it with Your Reverence, that if a happier day should perchance dawn again for our family, and we should return to the Capital, I may receive it from your hand once more?" At this the Abbot was much moved and replied with the following stanza:

> Since you cannot stay,
> Leave the Biwa here with me
> In its bag apart.
> Untouched by another hand,
> 'Twill recall the love you feel.

Tsunemasa returns the lute Seizan to the Imperial
Abbot of Ninnaji.

Tsunemasa, borrowing his master's inkstone, then wrote the following:

> Though the trickling stream
> That runs from this bamboo spout
> Changes ceaselessly,
> Never changing is my wish
> In these halls to stay with you.

When he had said farewell and retired from the presence of the Imperial Abbot, all those who were living in the monastery, acolytes, monks, and priests of all ranks, flocked round him, clinging to his sleeves and bedewing them with their tears, so sad were they at parting with him.

Among them was a certain young priest named Dainagon-no-Hoshi Gyōkei, a son of Hamuro-no-Dainagon Mitsuyori-no-Kyō, who had been much attached to him ever since his boyhood; and he was so loath to part with him that he went to see him off as far as the banks of the Katsuragawa, where he bade him farewell and returned to the monastery. As he parted with him, weeping he composed the following verse:

> Nature too is sad.
> See the mountain cherry-tree,
> Whether old or young,
> Whether late or early bud,
> Cannot keep its blossom long.

To which Tsunemasa made reply:

> In our traveller's garb,
> As we wend our weary way,
> Each night's bivouac
> Fills our hearts with saddening thoughts
> As we ever farther go.

Then his samurai, who had been waiting in groups here and there, unfurled their red banners and formed into a company of about a hundred horsemen in all, and as he took his place at their head they all whipped up their horses and galloped on after the Imperial Procession.

CONCERNING "SEIZAN"

It was when he was seventeen years old that Tsune-masa was presented with the Biwa "Seizan," and about the same time he was sent as Imperial Envoy to the shrine of Hachiman at Usa. When he arrived there he played certain secret pieces of great beauty on it before the abode of the deity, and all the assembled priests were so touched that the sleeves of their ritual garments were wet with their tears. Even those without any discrimination, who had never had any opportunity of hearing good music, were delighted, thinking it sounded like showers of rain.

And the story of this Biwa is that, when in the time of Nimmyō Tennō, in the third month of the third year of the period of Ka-shō, Kamon-no-kami Sadatoshi went to China, he learned three styles of playing from Renshō-bu, a very renowned master of the Biwa, and before he came back to Japan he was presented with three Biwas called "Genshō," "Shishi-maru," and "Seizan." But while he was returning over the sea, the Dragon god of the waters was moved by envy to raise a great storm, so they cast Shishi-maru into the waves to appease him, and brought back only two to this country, which were presented to the Emperor.

Many years after, in the period Ō-wa, the Emperor Murakami Tennō was sitting in the Seiryōden one autumn at midnight, when the moon was shining brightly and a cool breeze was blowing, and was playing on the Biwa called Genshō, when suddenly a shadowy form appeared before him and began to sing in a loud and sonorous voice. On the Emperor asking him who he was and whence he had come, he answered thus.

"I am Renshō-bu, that master of the Biwa who in China taught the three secret styles of playing to Fujiwara Sadatoshi; but in my teaching there was one tune that I concealed and did not transmit to him, and for this fault I have been cast into the place of devils. Having this night heard the wondrous beauty of your playing, I have come to ask Your Majesty if I may transmit the one remaining tune to you, and thus be permitted to enter the perfect enlightenment of Buddha." Then, taking Seizan which was standing before His Majesty also, he tuned the strings and taught the melody to the Emperor. And this is that which is called "Jogen" and "Sekijo."

After this apparition the Emperor and his Ministers feared to play on this Biwa, and it was presented to the Imperial Temple of Ninnaji, and Tsunemasa received it because he was so much beloved by the Imperial Abbot. The front of it was made of a rare wood, and on it was a picture of the moon of dawn coming forth from among the green foliage of summer mountains, hence its name Seizan (Green Mountain).

The Death of Kiso Yoshinaka

Now Kiso had brought with him from Shinano two beautiful girls named Tomoe and Yamabuki, but Yamabuki had fallen sick and stayed behind in the Capital. Tomoe had long black hair and a fair complexion, and her face was very lovely; moreover she was a fearless rider whom neither the fiercest horse nor the roughest ground could dismay, and so dexterously did she handle sword and bow that she was a match for a thousand warriors, and fit to meet either god or devil. Many times had she taken the field, armed at all points, and won matchless renown in encounters with the bravest captains, and so in this last fight, when all the others had been slain or had fled, among the last seven there rode Tomoe.

At first it was reported that Kiso had escaped to the north either through Nagasaka by the road to Tamba, or by the Ryūge Pass, but actually he had turned back again and ridden off toward Seta, to see if he could hear aught of the fate of Imai Kanehira. Imai had long valiantly held his position at Seta till the continued assaults of the enemy reduced his eight hundred men to but fifty, when he rolled up his banner and rode back to Miyako to ascertain the fate of his lord; and thus it happened that the two fell in with each other by the shore at Ōtsu. Recognizing each other when they were yet more than a hundred yards away, they spurred their horses and came together joyfully.

Seizing Imai by the hand, Kiso burst forth: "I was so anxious about you that I did not stop to fight to the death in the Rokujō-kawara, but turned my back on a host of foes and hastened off here to find you." "How can I express my gratitude for my lord's consideration?" replied Imai; "I too would have died in the defence of Seta, but I feared for my lord's uncertain fate, and thus it was that I fled hither." "Then our ancient pledge will not be broken and we shall die together," said Kiso, "and now unfurl your banner, for a sign to our men who have scattered among these hills."

So Imai unfurled the banner, and many of their men who had fled from the Capital and from Seta saw it and rallied again, so that they soon had a following of three hundred horse. "With this band our last fight will be a great one," shouted Kiso joyfully, "who leads yon great array?" "Kai-no-Ichijō Jirō, my lord." "And how many has he, do you think?" "About six thousand, it seems." "Well matched!" replied Yoshinaka, "if we must die, what death could be better than to fall outnumbered by valiant enemies? Forward then!"

That day Kiso was arrayed in a hitatare of red brocade and a suit of armour laced with Chinese silk; by his side hung a magnificent sword mounted in silver and gold, and his helmet was surmounted by long golden horns. Of his twenty-four eagle-feathered arrows, most had been shot away in the previous fighting, and only a few were left, drawn out high from the quiver, and he grasped his rattan-bound bow by the middle as he sat his famous grey charger, fierce as a devil, on a saddle mounted in gold. Rising high in his stirrups he cried with a loud voice: "Kiso-no-Kwanja you have often heard of; now you see him before your eyes! Lord of Iyo and Captain of the Guard, Bright Sun General, Minamoto Yoshinaka am I! Come! Kai-no-Ichijō Jirō! Take my head and show it to Hyōye-no-suke Yoritomo!"

"Hear, men!" shouted Ichijō-no-Jirō in response; "On to the attack! This is their great Captain! See that he does not escape you now!" And the whole force charged against Kiso to take him. Then Kiso and his three hundred fell upon their six thousand opponents in the death fury, cutting and slashing and swinging their blades in every direction until at last they broke through on the farther side, but with their little band depleted to only fifty horsemen, when Doino-Jirō Sanehira came up to support their foes with another force of two thousand. Flinging themselves on these they burst through them also, after which they successively penetrated several other smaller bands of a hundred or two who were following in reserve.

But now they were reduced to but five survivors, and among these Tomoe still held her place. Calling her to him Kiso said: "As you are a woman, it were better that you now make your escape. I have made up my mind to die, either by the hand of the enemy or by mine own, and how would Yoshinaka be shamed if in his last fight he died with a woman?" Even at these strong words, however, Tomoe would not forsake him, but still feeling full of fight, she replied: "Ah, for some bold warrior to match with, that Kiso might see how fine a death I can die." And she drew aside her horse and waited. Presently Onda-no-Hachirō Moroshige of Musashi, a strong and valiant samurai, came riding up with thirty followers, and Tomoe, immediately dashing into them, flung herself upon Onda and grappling with him dragged him from his horse, pressed him calmly against the pommel of her saddle and cut off his head. Then stripping off her armour she fled away to the Eastern Provinces.

Tezuka-no-Tarō was killed and Tezuka-no-Bettō took to flight, leaving Kiso alone with Imai-no-Shirō. "Ah," exclaimed Yoshinaka, "my armour that I am never wont to feel at all seems heavy on me to-day." "But you are not yet tired, my lord, and your horse is still fresh, so why should your armour feel heavy? If it is because you are discouraged at having none of your retainers left, remember that I, Kanehira, am equal to a thousand horsemen, and I have yet seven or eight arrows left in my quiver; so let me hold back the foe while my lord escapes to that pinewood of Awazu that we see yonder, that there under the trees he may put an end to his life in peace."

"Was it for this that I turned my back on my enemies in Rokujō-kawara and did not die then?" returned Yoshinaka; "by no means will we part now, but meet our fate together." And he reined his horse up beside that of Imai towards the foe, when Kanehira, alighting from his horse, seized his master's bridle and burst into tears: "However great renown a warrior may have gained," he pleaded, "an unworthy death is a lasting shame. My lord is weary and his charger also, and if, as may be, he meet his death at the hands of some low retainer, how disgraceful that it should be said that Kiso Dono, known through all Nippon as the 'Demon Warrior' had been slain by some nameless fellow, so listen to reason, I pray you, and get away to the pines over there."

So Kiso, thus persuaded, rode off toward the pine-wood of Awazu. Then Imai-no-Shirō, turning back, charged into a party of fifty horsemen, shouting: "I am Imai Shirō Kanehira, foster-brother of Kiso Dono, aged thirty-three. Even Yoritomo at Kamakura knows my name; so take my head and show it to him, anyone who can!" And he quickly fitted the eight shafts he had left to his bow and sent them whirring into the enemy, bringing down eight of them from their horses, either dead or wounded. Then, drawing his sword, he set on at the rest, but none would face him in combat hand-to-hand: "Shoot him down! Shoot him down!" they cried as they let fly a hail of arrows at him, but so good was his armour that none could pierce it, and once more he escaped unwounded.

Meanwhile Yoshinaka rode off alone toward Awazu, and it was the twenty-third day of the first month. It was now nearly dark and all the land was coated with thin ice, so that none could distinguish the deep rice-fields, and he had not gone far before his horse plunged heavily into the muddy ooze beneath. Right up to the neck it floundered, and though Kiso plied whip and spur with might and main, it was all to no purpose, for he could not stir it. Even in this plight he still thought of his retainer, and was turning to see how it fared with Imai, when Miura-no-Ishida Jirō Tamehisa of Sagami rode up and shot an arrow that struck him in the face under his helmet. Then as the stricken warrior fell forward in his saddle so that his crest bowed over his horse's head, two of Ishida's retainers fell upon him and struck off his head.

Holding it high on the point of a sword Ishida shouted loudly: "Kiso Yoshinaka, known through the length and breadth of Nippon as the 'Demon Warrior,' has been killed by Miura-no-Ishida Jirō Tamehisa." Imai was still fighting when these words fell on his ears, but when he saw that his master was indeed slain he cried out: "Alas, for whom now have I to fight? See, you fellows of the East Country, I will show you how the mightiest champion in Nippon can end his life!" And he thrust the point of his sword in his mouth and flung himself headlong from his horse, so that he was pierced through and died.

Now the Heike had departed from the coast of Yashima in Sanuki the winter of the year before, and crossed over to the bay of Naniwa in Settsu and took up a position between Ichi-no-tani on the west, where they built a strong fortification, and the wood of Ikuta on the east, where the entrance to the fort was made. Between these points, at Fukuhara, Hyogo, Itayado and Suma were encamped all the forces of the eight provinces of the Sanyōdō and the six provinces of the Nankaidō, a total of a hundred thousand men in all.

The position at Ichi-no-tani had a narrow entrance with cliffs on the north and the sea on the south, while within it was very spacious. The cliffs rose high and steep, perpendicular as a standing screen, and from them to the shallows of the beach a strong breastwork was erected of wood and stone, well protected by palisades, while beyond it, in the deep water rode their great galleys like a floating shield. In the towers of the breastwork were stationed the stout soldiery of Shikoku and Kyūshū in full armour with bows and arrows in their hands, dense as the evening mists, while in front of the towers, ten or twelve deep, stood their horses, fully accoutred with saddle and trappings. Ceaseless was the roll of their war-drums; the might of their bows was like the crescent moon, and the gleam of their blades was as the shimmer of the hoarfrost in autumn, while their myriad red banners that flew aloft in the spring breezes rose to heaven like the flames of a conflagration.

About dusk on the fifth day the Genji started from Koyano and pressed on to attack the wood at Ikuta, and as the Heike looked out over Suzume-no-matsubara, Mikage-no-matsu and Koyano, they could see them pitching their camps everywhere, while the glow of their thousand watch-fires reddened the sky like the moon rising over the mountains. The fires that the Heike kindled also showed up the dark outline of the wood of Ikuta, and twinkled as they flared up like stars in the brightening sky; they reminded them of the glimmering fire-flies on the river-bank, so often the subject of their verse in the happy days gone by. So, as they beheld the Genji thus deliberately pitching their camps here and there, and feeding and resting their horses, they watched and wondered when they would be attacked, their hearts filled with disquiet.

At dawn on the sixth day Kurō Onzōshi Yoshitsune, dividing his ten thousand men into two companies, ordered Doi-no-Jirō Sanehira to make an attack on the western outlet of Ichi-no-tani with seven thousand, while he himself with the remaining three thousand horsemen went round by the Tango road to descend the pass of Hiyodorigoe to take them in the rear.

At this his men began to murmur to each other: "Every one knows the dangers of that place; if we must die, it were better to die facing the foe than to fall over a cliff and be killed. Does anyone know the way among these mountains?" "I know these mountains very well;" exclaimed Hirayama-no-Mushadokoro of Musashi, in answer to these mutterings. "But you were brought up in the Eastern Provinces, and this is the first time you have seen the mountains of the West," objected Yoshitsune, "so how can you guide us?" "That may be even as your Excellency says," replied Hirayama, "but just as a poet knows the cherry-blossoms of Yoshino and Hatsuse without seeing them, so does a proper warrior know the way to the rear of an enemy's castle!"

After this most audacious speech, a young samurai of eighteen years old named Beppu-no-Kotarō Kiyoshige of Musashi spoke up and said: "I have often been told by my father Yoshishige that whether you are hunting on the mountains or fighting an enemy, if you lose your way you must take an old horse, tie the reins and throw them on his neck, and then drive him on in front, and he

will always find a path." "Well spoken," said Yoshitsune, "they say an old horse will find the road even
when it is buried in snow!" So they took an old grey
horse, trapped him with a silver-plated saddle and a
well-polished bit, and tying the reins and throwing them
on his neck, drove him on in front of them, and so
plunged into the unknown mountains.

As it was the beginning of the second month, the snow
had melted here and there on the peaks and at times
they thought they saw flowers, while at times they
heard the notes of the bush-warbler of the valleys, and
were hidden from sight in the mist. As they ascended,
the snow-clad peaks towered white and glistening on
either side of them, and as they descended again into
the valleys, the cliffs rose green on either hand. The
pines hung down under their load of snow, and scarcely
could they trace the narrow and mossy path. When a
sudden gust blew down a cloud of snow-flakes, they
almost took them for the falling plum-blossom. Whipping up their steeds to their best pace they rode on
some distance, until the falling dusk compelled them to
bivouac for the night in the depth of the mountains.

As they were thus halted, Musashi-bō Benkei suddenly appeared with an old man he had intercepted. In
answer to the questions of Yoshitsune he declared that
he was a hunter who lived in these mountains, and that
he knew all that country very well. "Then," said Yoshitsune, "what do you think of my plan of riding down
into Ichi-no-tani, the stronghold of the Heike?" "Ah,"
replied the old man, "that can hardly be done. The
valley is a hundred yards deep, and of that about half is

steep cliff where no one can go. Besides, the Heike will have dug pitfalls and spread caltrops inside the stronghold to make it impossible for your horses."

"Indeed?" returned Yoshitsune, "but is it possible for a stag to pass there?" "That stags pass there is certain," replied the hunter, "for in the warm days of spring they come from Harima to seek the thick pasture of Tamba, and when the winter grows cold they go back towards Inamino in Harima where the snow lies lighter." "Forsooth!" ejaculated Yoshitsune, "then a horse can do it, for where a stag may pass, there a horse can go also. Will you then be our guide?" "I am an old man now; how can I go so far?" replied the hunter. "But you have a son?" "I have." And Kumaō Maru, a youth of eighteen soon appeared before the Genji leader.

Then Yoshitsune performed the ceremony of Gempuku for the young man, giving him the name of Washio Saburō Yoshihisa, the name of his father being Washio Shōji Takehisa, and he accompanied them, going on in front to guide them down into Ichi-no-tani. And after the Heike had been overthrown and the Genji obtained the supremacy, and his lord Yoshitsune fell into disfavour with his brother and fled to Mutsu and fell there, Washio Saburō Yoshihisa was one of those who followed him to the death.

THE DESCENT OF THE HILL

Thereafter the battle became general and the various clans of the Gen and Hei surged over each other in mixed and furious combat. The men of the Miura,

Kamakura, Chichibu, Ashikaga, Noiyo, Yokoyama, Inomata, Kodama, Nishi Tsuzuki and Kisaichi clans charged against each other with a roar like thunder, while the hills re-echoed to the sound of their war-cries, and the shafts they shot at each other fell like rain. Some were wounded slightly and fought on, some grappled and stabbed each other to death, while others bore down their adversaries and cut off their heads: everywhere the fight rolled forward and backward, so that none could tell who were victors or vanquished.

Thus it did not appear that the main body of the Genji had been successful in their attack, when at dawn on the seventh day Kurō Onzōshi Yoshitsune with his force of three thousand horsemen, having climbed to the top of the Hiyodorigoe, was resting his horses before the descent. Just then, startled by the movements of his men, two stags and a doe rushed out and fled over the cliff straight into the camp of the Heike.

"That is strange," exclaimed the Heike men-at-arms, "for the deer of this part ought to be frightened at our noise and run away to the mountains. Aha! it must be the enemy who is preparing to drop on us from above!" And they began to run about in confusion, when forth strode Takechi-no-Mushadokoro of the province of Iyo, and drawing his bow transfixed the two stags, though letting the doe escape. "Thus," he cried, "will we deal with any who try that road, and none are likely to pass it alive!" "What useless shooting of stags is this?" said Etchū Zenji Moritoshi when he saw it; "one of those arrows might have stopped ten of the enemy, so why waste them in that fashion?"

Then Yoshitsune, looking down on the Heike position from the top of the cliff, ordered some horses to be driven down the declivity, and of these, though some missed their footing half-way, and breaking their legs, fell to the bottom and were killed, three saddled horses scrambled down safely and stood, trembling in every limb, before the residence of Etchū Zenji. "If they have riders to guide them," said Yoshitsune, "the horses will get down without damage, so let us descend, and I will show you the way;" and he rode over the cliff at the head of his thirty retainers, seeing which the whole force of three thousand followed on after him.

For more than a hundred yards the slope was sandy with small pebbles, so that they slid straight down it and landed on a level place, from which they could survey the rest of the descent. From thence downwards it was all great mossy boulders, but steep as a well, and some fifty yards to the bottom. It seemed impossible to go on any farther, neither could they now retrace their steps, and the soldiers were recoiling in horror, thinking that their end had come, when Miura-no-Sahara Jūrō Yoshitsura sprang forward and shouted: "In my part we ride down places like this any day to catch a bird; the Miura would make a racecourse of this;" and down he went, followed by all the rest.

So steep was the descent that the stirrups of the hinder man struck against the helmet or armour of the one in front of him, and so dangerous did it look that

Minamoto Yoshitsune rides down Hiyodori Pass.

they averted their eyes as they went down. "Ei! Ei!" they ejaculated under their breath as they steadied their horses, and their daring seemed rather that of demons than of men. So they reached the bottom, and as soon as they found themselves safely down they burst forth with a mighty shout, which echoed along the cliffs so that it sounded rather like the battle-cry of ten thousand men than of three.

Then Murakami-no-Hangwan-dai Yasukuni seized a torch and fired the houses and huts of the Heike so that they went up in smoke in a few moments, and when their men saw the clouds of black smoke rising they at once made a rush toward the sea, if haply they might find a way of escape. There was no lack of ships drawn up by the beach, but in their panic four or five hundred men in full armour and even a thousand all crowded into one ship, so that when they had rowed out not more than fifty or sixty yards from the shore, three large ships turned over and sank before their eyes.

Moreover those in the ships would only take on board those warriors who were of high rank, and thrust away the common soldiers, slashing at them with their swords and halberds, but even though they saw this, rather than stay and be cut down by the enemy, they clung to the ships and strove to drag themselves on board, so that their hands and arms were cut off and they fell back into the sea, which quickly reddened with their blood.

Thus, both on the main front and on the sea-shore did the young warriors of Musashi and Sagami strain every nerve in the fight, caring nothing for their lives as they rushed desperately to the attack. What must have been the feelings of Noto-no-kami Noritsune, who in all his many battles had never been vanquished until now? Mounting his charger Usuzumi, he galloped away toward the west, and taking ship from Takasago in Harima, crossed over to Yashima in Sanuki.

THE DEATH OF TADANORI

Satsuma-no-kami Tadanori, the Commander of the western army, clad in a dark-blue hitatare and a suit of armour with black silk lacing, and mounted on a great black horse with a saddle enriched with lacquer of powdered gold, was calmly withdrawing with his following of a hundred horsemen, when Okabe-no-Rokuyata Tadazumi of Musashi espied him and pursued at full gallop, eager to bring down so noble a prize.

"This must be some great leader!" he cried. "Shameful! to turn your back to the foe!" Tadanori turned in the saddle; "We are friends! We are friends!" he replied, as he continued on his way. As he had turned, however, Tadazumi had caught a glimpse of his face and noticed that his teeth were blackened. "There are none of our side who have blackened teeth," he said, "this must be one of the Heike Courtiers." And overtaking him, he ranged up to him to grapple. When his hundred followers saw this, since they were hired retainers drawn from various provinces, they scattered and fled in all directions, leaving their leader to his fate.

But Satsuma-no-kami, who had been brought up at Kumano, was famous for his strength, and was extremely active and agile besides, so clutching Tadazumi he pulled him from his horse, dealing him two stabs with his dirk while he was yet in the saddle, and following them with another as he was falling. The first two blows fell on his armour and failed to pierce it, while the third wounded him in the face but was not mortal, and as Tadanori sprang down upon him to cut off his head, Tadazumi's page, who had been riding behind him, slipped from his horse and with a blow of his sword cut off Tadanori's arm above the elbow.

Satsuma-no-kami, seeing that all was over and wishing to have a short space to say the death-prayer, flung Tadazumi from him so that he fell about a bow's length away. Then turning toward the west he repeated: "Kōmyō Henjō Jippō Sekai, Nembutsu Shujō Sesshu Fusha; O Amida Nyorai, who sheddest the light of Thy Presence through the ten quarters of the world, gather into Thy Radiant Heaven all who call upon Thy Name!" And just as his prayer was finished, Tadazumi from behind swept off his head.

Not doubting that he had taken the head of a noble foe, but quite unaware who he might be, he was searching his armour when he came across a piece of paper fastened to his quiver, on which was written a verse with this title: "The Traveller's Host, a Flower."

> Now the daylight dies,
> And the shadow of a tree
> Serves me for an inn.
> For the host to welcome me
> There is but a wayside flower.

Wherefore he knew that it could be none but Satsuma-no-kami.

Then he lifted up the head on his sword's point and shouted with a loud voice: "Satsuma-no-kami Dono, the demon-warrior of Nippon, slain by Okabe-Roku-yata Tadazumi of Musashi!" And when they heard it, all, friends and foes alike, moistened the sleeves of their armour with their tears exclaiming: "Alas! what a great captain has passed away! Warrior and artist and poet; in all things he was pre-eminent."

Shigehira is Taken Alive

Hon-sammi Chūjō Shigehira was second in command at Ikuta-no-mori, and he was attired that day in a hitatare of dark-blue cloth on which a pattern of rocks and sea-birds was embroidered in light yellow silk, and armour with purple lacing deepening in its hue toward the skirts. On his head was a helmet with tall golden horns, and his sword also was mounted in gold. His arrows were feathered with black and white falcon plumes, and in his hand he carried a "Shigeto" bow. He was mounted on a renowned war-horse called Dōji-kage, whose trappings were resplendent with ornaments of gold. With him was his foster-brother Gotō Hyōye Morinaga in a hitatare of dyed brocade and a suit of armour with scarlet lacing, and he too was mounted on a splendid cream-coloured charger named Yome-nashi.

As they were riding along the shore to take ship and escape, Shō-no-Shirō Takaie and Kajiwara Genda

Kagesue, thinking they looked a fine prize, spurred on their horses and bore down upon them. Now there were many ships ranged along the shore, but the enemy pressed on them so hard from behind that there was no opportunity to embark, so the two, crossing the Minatogawa and the Karumogawa, and leaving Hasu-no-ike on the right and Koma-no-hayashi on the left, rode hard through Itayado and Suma and endeavoured to make their escape to the west.

As Shigehira was mounted on such a famous charger as Dōji-kage it seemed unlikely that any ordinary horse would overhaul him, and the pursuers mounts were already weakening, when Kajiwara drew his bow to the head and sent an arrow whizzing after them. Though a long venture the shaft flew true to its mark, and buried itself deeply in the hind-leg of the Chūjō's steed, just above the root of the tail. Seeing its pace slacken his foster-brother Morinaga, thinking that the Chūjō might demand his mount, whipped it up and made good his escape. "Ah!" exclaimed the Chūjō, "why do you desert me thus? Have you forgotten all your promises?" But he paid no heed, and tearing off the red badge from his armour, thought of nothing but saving himself by flight. Then the Chūjō, seeing that his horse could go no farther, plunged headlong into the sea to die by drowning, but the water was so shallow that there was no time, and as he started to cut himself open, Shō-no-Shirō Takaie rode up, and springing from his horse, called out to him: "Desist I pray you; allow me to take you with me." And placing him on his own horse, he bound him to the pommel of his saddle and escorted him back to the Genji camp.

The Chūjō's foster-brother Morinaga, who had ridden away and deserted him, fled to seek refuge with Onaka Hōkyō, one of the priests of Kumano, but after his death returned again to the Capital with his widow, when she came up on account of a lawsuit that she had. There he was recognized by many of his associates who had known him in past times, and they pointed the finger of scorn at him saying: "How disgraceful! There is Gotō Hyōye Morinaga, who deserted the Chūjō in his need and refused to aid him. He has come back again with the widow of the Hōkyō." And Morinaga, when he heard it was so ashamed that he hid his face with his fan.

THE DEATH OF ATSUMORI

Now when the Heike were routed at Ichi-no-tani, and their Nobles and Courtiers were fleeing to the shore to escape in their ships, Kumagai Jirō Naozane came riding along a narrow path on to the beach, with the intention of intercepting one of their great captains. Just then his eye fell on a single horseman who was attempting to reach one of the ships in the offing, and had swum his horse out some twenty yards from the water's edge.

He was richly attired in a silk hitatare embroidered with storks, and the lacing of his armour was shaded green; his helmet was surmounted by lofty horns, and the sword he wore was gay with gold. His twenty-four arrows had black and white feathers, and he carried a black-lacquered bow bound with rattan. The horse he rode was dappled grey, and its saddle glittered with gold-mounting. Not doubting that he was one of the chief captains, Kumagai beckoned to him with his war-fan, crying out: "Shameful! to show an enemy your back. Return! Return!"

Then the warrior turned his horse and rode him back to the beach, where Kumagai at once engaged him in mortal combat. Quickly hurling him to the ground, he sprang upon him and tore off his helmet to cut off his head, when he beheld the face of a youth of sixteen or seventeen, delicately powdered and with blackened teeth, just about the age of his own son, and with features of great beauty. "Who are you?" he inquired; "Tell me your name, for I would spare your life." "Nay, first say who you are;" replied the young man. "I am Kumagai Jirō Naozane of Musashi, a person of no particular importance." "Then you have made a good capture;" said the youth. Take my head and show it to some of my side and they will tell you who I am."

"Though he is one of their leaders," mused Kumagai, "if I slay him it will not turn defeat into victory, and if I spare him, it will not turn victory into defeat. When my son Kojirō was but slightly wounded at Ichino-tani, did it not make my heart bleed? How pitiful then to put this youth to death." And so he was about to set him free, when, looking behind him, he saw Doi and Kajiwara coming up with fifty horsemen. "Alas! look there," he exclaimed, the tears running down his face, "though I would spare your life, the whole countryside swarms with our men, and you cannot escape them. If you must die, let it be by my hand, and I will see that prayers are said for your rebirth in bliss." "Indeed it must be," said the young warrior, "so take off my head at once."

Then Kumagai, weeping bitterly, and so overcome by his compassion for the fair youth that his eyes swam and his hand trembled so that he could scarcely wield his blade, hardly knowing what he did, at last cut off his head. "Alas!" he cried, "what life is so hard as that of a soldier? Only because I was born of a warrior family must I suffer this affliction! How lamentable it is to do such cruel deeds!" And he pressed his face to the sleeve of his armour and wept bitterly. Then, wrapping up the head, he was stripping off the young man's armour, when he discovered a flute in a brocade bag that he was carrying in his girdle.

"Ah," he exclaimed, "it was this youth and his friends who were diverting themselves with music within the walls this morning. Among all our men of the Eastern Provinces I doubt if there is any who has brought a flute with him. What esthetes are these Courtiers of the Heike!" And when he brought them and showed them to the Commander, all who saw them were moved to tears; and he then discovered that the youth was Taiyū-Atsumōri, the youngest son of Shūri-no-taiyū Tsunemori, aged seventeen years. From this time the mind of Kumagai was turned toward the religious life and he eventually became a recluse.

The flute of Atsumōri was one which his grandfather Tadanori, who was a famous player, had received as a present from the Emperor Toba, and had handed down to his father Tsunemori, who had given it to Atsumōri because of his skill on the instrument. It was called "Saeda."* Concerning this story of Kumagai we may quote the saying that "even in the most droll and flippant farce there is the germ of a Buddhist Psalm."†

Thus as the day wore on both Genji and Heike fell in great numbers at the eastern and western barriers, and before the towers and beneath the barricades the bodies of men and horses lay in heaps, while the green grass of Ichi-no-tani and Osasahara was turned to crimson. Countless were those who fell by arrow and sword at Ichi-no-tani and Ikuta-no-mori, by the hillside and by the strand of the sea. Two thousand heads did the Genji take in this battle, and of the Courtiers of the Heike, Echizen-no-Sammi Michimori, his younger brother Kurando-no-taiyū Narimori, Satsuma-no-kami Tadanori, Musashi-no-kami Tomoakira, Bitchū-no-kami Moromori, Owari-no-kami Kiyosada, Awaji-no-kami Kiyofusa, Kōgō-gū-no-suke Tsunemasa the eldest son of Tsunemori, his younger brother Wakasa-no-kami Tsunetoshi, and his younger brother Taiyū Atsumōri, beside ten others, all fell at Ichi-no-tani.

When their stronghold was thus captured, the Heike were compelled to put to sea once more, taking the

---

*Little branch.

†i.e. How much more does a serious incident like this turn the mind to religion.

child Emperor with them. Some of their vessels were driven by wind and tide toward the province of Kii, while others rowed and tossed about, buffeted by the waves, in the offing of Ashiya. Some rocked on the billows off Suma and Akashi, steering aimlessly hither and thither, their crews weary and dispirited as they turned on their hard plank couches, and viewed the moon of spring mistily through their tear-dimmed eyes.

Some crossed the straits of Awaji and drifted along by Ejima-ga-Iso, likening their lot to the sad sea-birds that fly there seeking by twilight the mate they have lost, while others still lay off Ichi-no-tani uncertain where to steer. Yesterday, with a host of a hundred thousand, feared and obeyed by fourteen provinces, they lay with high hopes but one day's journey from the Capital, and now, after the defeat of Ichi-no-tani, they were scattered and dispersed along the coast, each unaware of the fate of his friend.

MICHIMORI'S WIFE DROWNS HERSELF

Now Kenda Takiguchi Tokikazu, a retainer of Echizen-no-Sammi Michimori, fled in haste to the ship in which was the wife of Michimori, and said to her: "This morning my lord was surrounded by seven horsemen at the Minatogawa and fell fighting, and among them were Sasaki-no-Kimura Saburō Naritsuna of Ōmi, and Tamai-no-Shirō Sukekage of Musashi. I too would have stayed with him to the end and died, but he had strictly charged me before, saying that if anything should happen to him I must at all costs escape to look after my mistress; and so it is that I have saved my worthless life and come to you."

On hearing these tidings his mistress uttered no word, but covered her face and fell prostrate. Though she had already heard that he was dead, she had not at first believed it, but for two or three days had waited as for one who had gone out for a short time and would soon come back. However, when four or five days had passed, her confidence was shaken, and she fell into deep melancholy. Her feelings were shared by her foster-mother who alone accompanied her and shared the same pillow.

From the seventh day, on which the news was brought to her, until the evening of the thirteenth she did not rise from her bed. At dawn on the fourteenth day the Heike were starting to cross again to Yashima, and until the evening before she still lay on her couch. Then as night drew on and all was quiet in the ship, she turned to her foster-mother and said: "Though I had been told it, until this morning I did not realize that my husband was dead, but now, this evening, I know it is true. Every one says he was killed at the Minatogawa, and after that there is none who says he has seen him alive. And what grieves me most is that when I saw him for a short while on the night before the battle he was sad and said to me: 'I am certain to be slain in to-morrow's battle, and I wonder what will become of you after I am gone.' As there have been so many battles I did not pay any special heed to it, but if I had thought that it was the last time indeed, I would have promised to follow him to the after world.

"Then, fearing that he might think me too reserved, I told him what I had up till that time concealed, that I was 'not alone.' He was extremely pleased to hear it and said: 'Ah, I have reached thirty years of age without having any children; I hope you will make it a boy if you can, for that will be a good memento of myself to leave behind in this fleeting world.' Then he went on to ask me how many months it was, and how I felt, and bade me keep as quiet as was possible in this ever-rolling ship that the birth might be easy.

"Ah, how sad it all is! If women die at that time it is a most shameful and melancholy end that they suffer, and yet, if I bear this child and bring it up so that it may recall to me the features of him who is gone, every time I look on it it will bring back the memory of my former love, and that will cause me grief without end. Death is the road that none may avoid. Even if I should by good luck pass scatheless through these dangerous times, can I trust myself to escape the common fate of being entangled in some other passion? That too is a melancholy prospect. To behold him in my dreams when I sleep, and to awake only to look on his features! Better to drown in the depths of the sea than to live on thus bereft of my love. My heart is full of sorrow at leaving you thus alone, but I pray you send to Miyako this letter which I have written, and take my robes to some priest, that his prayers may hasten the enlightenment of my husband, and may assist me too in the after world."

When she had made an end of speaking, the older woman, repressing her tears, replied: "How can you thus resolve to forsake your little one and leave your mother alone in her old age? Is your loss any greater than that of the other wives of the nobles of our house who have fallen at Ichi-no-tani? Though you may think you will sit on the same lotus as your husband, yet after rebirth you must both pass through the Six Ways and the Four Births, and in which of these can you be sure of meeting? And if you fail to meet, of what use is it to cast away your life? So be brave and calm your mind until your child is born, and strive to bring it up, whatever hardships may threaten. Then you may become a nun and spend your days in prayer for the happy rebirth of your departed husband. Moreover, as for Miyako, who is there who can carry such a letter?"

Then the lady, wishing to comfort and reassure her weeping parent, replied: "If I seem strange, you must remember that under the stress of misfortune or the pain of parting to think of ending one's life is a natural thing, though really to nerve oneself to do so is not so easy; and if I should indeed resolve to carry out this intention I will be sure to let you know. But now it is late and I would sleep."

Now her foster-mother, seeing that the lady had not even taken a bath for the last four or five days, concluded that her mind was indeed made up, and had herself determined that if she did so she would follow her even to the bottom of the sea, for she did not wish to live a day longer if her daughter was dead, so for some time she remained awake watching by her side, but at last she fell asleep, whereupon the lady, who had been awaiting this opportunity, slipped out quietly and ran to the bulwarks of the ship.

Gazing out over the wide expanse of waters, she was uncertain in which direction lay the western quarter, but turning toward the setting moon as it was sinking behind the mountains, calmly she repeated the Nembutsu. The melancholy cry of the sea-birds on the distant sand-spits and the harsh creaking of the rudder mingled with her voice as she repeated it a hundred times. "Namu Amida Nyorai, Saviour who leadest us to the Western Paradise, according to Thy True Vow unite on the same lotus flower an inseparable husband and wife!" And with the last invocation still on her lips she cast herself into the waves.

It was about midnight of the day on which they were to start for Yashima, and all aboard the ship were sleeping soundly, so no one perceived her. But as she plunged into the waves she attracted the attention of the helmsman, who alone of the crew was not asleep, and he cried out loudly that a woman had gone over-board from the ship, whereon the foster-mother, sud-denly awakening, felt by her side, and finding nothing, was overcome by sorrow and amazement. Then, though all did their utmost to get her out of the water and save her life, as usual in spring, the sky was cloudy and the moon obscured so that they could not see where she was, and when at last they did discover her and pull her out of the water, her life was already departing.

Thus they laid her on the deck with the salt water

Michimori's wife drowns herself.

streaming from her white hakama and the thick double layers of her Court costume, and dripping from her long black hair, and her foster-mother, taking her hands in hers and pressing her face to her cold features, exclaimed: "Why did you not let me know your resolve, and let me follow you to the bottom of the sea? Woe is me, now I am left here all alone! At least will you not speak to me once more?" But though she thus addressed her daughter in tones of agonized entreaty, she was already destined for that other world, and her breath, which until now had just barely fluttered in her body, at last departed for ever.

SENSHU

Now Sammi Chūjō Shigehira was brought into the presence of Yoritomo who thus addressed him: "To appease the Imperial displeasure, and to wipe away the stain from my father's memory I have undertaken to overthrow the Heike family, and it will not be difficult to accomplish; but verily I did not at all expect to see you here under these circumstances. As it is, perchance I may have the honour of receiving Munemori as well. But concerning the burning of the temples of Nara, whether it was done by the command of the late Chancellor Kiyomori, or whether it was ordered by you on the spur of the moment, I know not; but anyhow it was an exceeding heinous crime."

"It was done neither by the command of the Chancellor nor by my own design," replied the Chūjō, "but it happened accidentally in the course of the operations

we undertook to suppress the violence of the monks.
I beg your indulgence to speak of a fresh subject, but,
as you know, in former days the Genji and Heike
families stood together in rivalry to support the
Throne, and after that the fortunes of the Genji house
declined, and our family alone, since the days of Hogen
and Heiji, has many times subdued the Imperial
enemies, and been rewarded for its services, even, I
speak it with reverence, so far as to be permitted to become Imperial Relatives, and to hold the office of Chief
Minister; while no less than sixty members of the
family have been promoted to high office, so that for
twenty years there has been none to equal it in all the
land for rank and authority.

Now it is said that he who fights the battles of the
Emperor shall not be bereft of the Imperial Favour
for seven generations; but this I think is quite false,
for though the late Chancellor hazarded his life for the
Throne many times, it was his generation only that
was fortunate and happy, and his children have come
to this state that you behold. Our fate has come upon
us and our rule is overthrown: fugitives from the
Capital, our corpses bleach on mountain and plain, and
men would spread our shame far over the waves of the
Western Ocean. That I should thus be taken alive and
brought down hither is a thing of which I never
dreamed, and I can but regard it as the result of the
misdeeds of a former life. In the history of China it is
related that King T'ang of Yin was imprisoned at
Hsia T'ai and Wen Wang was held captive at Yu Li'.

And if there were such examples in antiquity, how
should the men of this age fare better? It is not really
such a disgrace for a warrior to fall into the hands of
his enemy and be put to death, so I pray you of your
favour grant me a speedy execution."

As he thus finished speaking, Kajiwara exclaimed
in admiration: "Ah! There is a great leader indeed!
And both he and the samurai in attendance could not
refrain from pressing their sleeves to their eyes.
Yoritomo too was not unaffected by his bearing. "Far
be it from me to regard the Taira house as my personal
foes," he exclaimed in reply, "it is only that I carry out
the Imperial Order: as for the burning of the temples
of the South Capital, let that be settled by the decision
of the monks themselves."

And he ordered that the Chūjō should be placed in
charge of Kanō-no-suke Munemochi of the province
of Izu. A treatment that seemed just like the handing
over of the sinners of the Shaba-world to the Ten
Kings for seven days each.   But this Kanō-no-suke
was a merciful man and did not treat the Chūjō at
all severely, but was very kind to him in all things.
And first of all he led him away to take a hot bath.
Now the Chūjō thought he could meet any fate calmly
if he could wash away the dust and grime of the road,
and make himself clean again, and was just taking his
bath, when after a little while the door of the bath-
room was opened and there entered a beautiful girl of
about twenty years old, with a fine white complexion
and very lovely hair.

She was wearing a bath-robe of unlined material

dyed in colours, and was attended by a little maid of
fourteen or fifteen with short hair, dressed in an
unlined garment of white, dyed with a blue design
here and there, and carrying some combs in a small
wash-basin. This lady assisted the Chūjō in his bath
for some time, and then, after she had washed her hair,
made to depart again, but as she was going out she
said to him: "I am one of those who have access to
Yoritomo, so if there is anything you wish, please tell
me, and I will ask him; it may be difficult for a man,
but a woman can manage these things."

"In this condition, what can I want?" replied the
Chūjō, "there is only one thing that I could desire, and
that is to be allowed to become a monk." This request
the lady repeated to Yoritomo, but he replied: "That
cannot be. If he were my own enemy, it might be, but
as he is an enemy of the Throne it is not possible."
When the lady brought this answer to the Chūjō, after
she had retired again he asked his guard what might
be the name of this very elegant visitor. "She is the
daughter of the Chōja of Tegoshi," said Kanō-no-suke,
"and she is equally winsome in face and figure and
disposition; she has been in attendance on the lord
Hyōye-no-suke for some two or three years, and her
name is Senshū-no-Mae."

That evening was somewhat rainy, and everything
was very dreary, when the lady again appeared bringing a lute and harp. Kanō-no-suke also came in with
ten of his attendants and brought wine before the
Chūjō, which Senshū-no-Mae served to him. Shigehira took a little, but seemed rather indifferent to their

attentions, whereupon Kanō-no-suke spoke as follows:
"I am a man of the province of Izu, and am only a
sojourner in Kamakura, but I will do anything I can
to serve you; and Hyōye-no-suke Dono has ordered
that we accede to any wishes you may have, so please
command us. So let *sake* be served."

So Senshū-no-Mae brought him *sake* and recited
once and again the piece entitled: "I am angry with
the weaving-woman for the heaviness of my silken
robe." "Though Kitano Tenjin, the Deity of Literature, swore that he would hasten three times a day to
protect him who sings this verse," said the Chūjō,
"seeing that I am one forsaken and without hope in
this world, of what avail is it to join in the singing;
still, if it will at all lessen my guilt, I will do so." Then
Senshū sang the refrain entitled: "Even the Ten
Transgressions, they shall be taken away," and then
sang four or five times the Imayō measure: "Let all
who desire Paradise call on the name of Amida."

Then the Chūjō drained his cup, and Senshū took
it and gave it to Kanō-no-suke, and while he was drink-
ing she played the lute. "This melody is usually called
Gojō-raku," said the Chūjō in jest; "but now it seems
to me like Goshō-raku (songs of the next world); so
I will sing the piece called Ōjō-no-kyū (hastening to
heaven): and he took the lute and tuned it, and sang
the melody Ōjō-no-kyū.

And so the night grew on, and his heart became free
of care, and he said: "Who would have thought to find
such grace in the Eastern Provinces? Let us have
another song." So Senshū-no-Mae sang several times

with great feeling the Shirabyōshi refrain: "Those who find shelter beneath one tree, or those who snatch a draught from the same stream; it is naught but the promise of a former life." Then the Chūjō also sang: "The tears of Yü Chi when the light grew dim." And the meaning of this song is as follows: when in old time in China the Emperor Kao Tsu of Han strove with Hsiang U of Ch'u, Hsiang U triumphed in seventy-two battles, but at length he was beaten and his army routed. Then, springing on to his horse Sui, famous for its wondrous strength and swiftness, he made to escape with his consort Yü Chi, when strange to say the horse set both his feet firm and refused to move. Shedding tears of chagrin Hsiang U exclaimed: "My power is already gone, and for the attacks of the enemy I care nothing, all that grieves me is the parting with this lady." It is the scene of Yü Chi weeping in the waning light, as the troops of the enemy came shouting down on all sides, that Tachibana Hiromi has represented in this poem, and it was a sign of the Chūjō's artistic feeling that he chose it to sing on this occasion.

So they went on until the day was about to break, when Kanō-no-suke took leave of the Chūjō, and Senshū-no-Mae returned also. That morning it chanced that Yoritomo was reading the Hokke Sutras in his private oratory when she came back, and he turned to her with a smile and remarked: "No doubt the entertainment last night was very amusing?" At this Sai-in-no-Jikwan Chikayoshi, who was writing something in his presence, asked what he meant. "For the last two or three years the Heike have experienced nothing but hardships and fighting," said Yoritomo, "and yet so charming was the playing and singing of Sammi Chūjō that I stood all night outside listening to it. He is indeed a fine artist."

"I too should have liked to hear it," replied Chikayoshi, "but I had some other business last night and so I could not; but I will take the first chance of doing so henceforth. The Heike have always produced many talented musicians and artists, and a while ago when they were comparing each other to various flowers, they decided that Sammi Chūjō was the peony among them." At any rate his playing the lute and singing so impressed Yoritomo that he never forgot it.

When Senshū-no-Mae afterwards heard that the Chūjō had been sent to Nara and put to death there, the tidings so affected her that she retired from the world and became a nun, entering the temple of Zenkōji in Shinano, there to pray for his happy rebirth in Paradise.

YOKOBUE

Now though the body of Komatsu-no-Sammi Chūjō Koremori was in Yashima, yet his heart was ever in Miyako, for never for a moment was his mind free from anxiety about his wife and little ones whom he had left in the Capital. Unable at last to bear the suspense, on the fifteenth day of the third month of the third year of Ju-ei he slipped out of his house at Yashima at dawn and departed, accompanied by Yosōhyōye Shigekage, his page Ishidō Maru, and an attendant named Takesato, who was included because he understood ships. With these three he took ship at Yuki-no-ura in the province of Awa, and after passing by the offing of Naruto, they shaped their course towards Kii, passing on their way the shrines of Tamatsu-shima Myōjin, Nichizen and Kokken, and arriving at last at Minato in Kii.

Thence he thought to go by the hills to Miyako and meet his wife and children, but when he remembered how his uncle the Chūjō Shigehira had been taken alive, and exposed to the shame of being carried thus to Miyako and Kamakura, he feared to heap shame on his father's grave if he also were taken, and though his feelings naturally dragged him in that direction, he fought them down and proceeded to Kōya.

Now in Kōya there was a certain saintly priest whom he had formerly known. He had been a retainer of Shigemori, and his name was Saitō Takiguchi Tokiyori, the son of Saitō Saemon Mochiyori. When he was thirteen years of age he had gone to the Palace to take up his duties, and there he fell deeply in love with a girl named Yokobue, a maid-in-waiting on the Imperial Consort Kenrei-mon-in. When his father heard of this he remonstrated with him very strongly, for he had intended that his son should make a good match through which he might be able to obtain a good position at Court.

Thereupon Takiguchi exclaimed: "In ancient times in China there lived one named Si Wang Mu who is alive no longer, and Tung Fang So also is now but a name and nothing more. Fleeting are the limits of youth and age; for as a flash of fire they pass and are gone. If we speak of long life, it is but seventy or eighty years, and of these the prime of life is no more than twenty. So in this world of dreams and illusions why be burdened with one we dislike, even for a moment? But if I look on the one I love it is disobedience to my father. By this lesson I will learn virtue. I will renounce this passing world and enter the way of Buddha."

And at the age of nineteen he shaved his head and entered the temple of Ōjō-in in Saga. When Yokobue heard this, she said: "That he should give me up is quite natural, but why be so foolish as to become a monk? And if he meant to retire from the world, why did he not first come and tell me of it?" So thinking that however strong his resolve might be, he might have come and expressed his regret, she left the city one evening and set off for Saga in anxious mood.

It was now past the tenth day of the second month, and the spring breeze of Umezu wafted her the grateful scent of many blossoms, while the moon, half-hidden by the drifting mist, reflected itself dimly in the Ōigawa, but how sad and troubled was her heart as she searched for her lover. All she had heard was the name of the temple, but she knew not in what part of it he was living, and so she wandered about distractedly hither and thither, trying to find it in great distress. Then she heard proceeding from a rough and poor cell the voice of some one reciting the Sutras, and she knew it for the voice of Takiguchi Nyūdō.

So she told the maid who was with her to go and take this message: "Even though you have thus changed your condition, I, Yokobue have come so far to see you once more." Takiguchi was greatly amazed and agitated to hear this, and peeping through a hole in the shōji, saw her standing outside, the skirts of her garments soaked with dew, and her sleeves wet with tears. Her face had grown thinner in the meanwhile, and she looked weary with her search, truly a sight to melt the heart of the most fanatic devotee. But Takiguchi only sent some one out to say: "The person whom you seek is not here. You must have come to the wrong place." And so there was nothing for Yokobue to do but to swallow her tears and wend her way back to Miyako, sad and bitter of heart.

By and by Takiguchi said to the monk who dwelt with him: "This is a quiet place, and there is no interruption to one's prayers, but now that girl knows my whereabouts, and though once I was able to steel my heart, if she should follow me again I might melt. Farewell." And he left Saga and betook himself to Mount Kōya, where he entered the temple of Shōjō-shin-in to practise the religious life. There after a while he heard that Yokobue too had left the world and become a nun, and he sent her this stanza:

> Till you shaved your head
> And vowed to renounce the world
> Your heart found no peace.
> Surely you must now be glad,
> Having entered Buddha's way.

To this Yokobue answered:

> Now I've shaved my head
> And become a cloistered nun,
> What should I regret?
> There can be no looking back
> Having entered Buddha's way.

Afterwards she entered the temple of Hokkeji at Nara, but she was unable to forget the past, and brooded over it until before long she fell sick and died. When Takiguchi Nyūdō was told of it he redoubled his religious austerities, and his father forgave his unfilial conduct, so that he became to be known to all who were acquainted with him as the Saint of Kōya.

Now when Koremori met him after a long while he remembered him as attired in Court costume, his hair carefully dressed and his whole appearance rich and gay, but the man he now beheld was dressed in a priest's robe and stole of sombre colour, and though he was not yet thirty years old, he looked like an emaciated old monk. His person exuded an odour of incense-smoke, and his whole demeanour was that of a sage sunk in profound and pious meditations, so much that his condition seemed to Koremori a most enviable one. Perhaps the Seven Sages of Tsin who dwelt in the Bamboo Grove, or the Four Greybeards of Han who lived in Shang Shan, did not look more venerable than he.

THE BOOK OF KŌYA

When Takiguchi Nyūdō saw that it was Koremori, he exclaimed: "Can it be that you are not an illusion? Then how is it that you have managed to escape from Yashima?" "When I left the Capital for the Western Provinces," replied Koremori, "I did not think much of it, but afterwards I could not rest for a moment for anxiety about those I had left behind there, and though I said nothing my feelings were apparent, and both Munemori and the Nii Dono were uncertain whether Yoritomo would extend to them the indulgence that he had to Yorimori for the sake of Ikeno-Zenni, and so, unable to bear the suspense any longer, I was impelled to come thus far. Here I thought to renounce the world, and yield up my life by fire or water, but I have a great desire to go to Kumano." "The affairs of this world of dreams are of little matter," replied Takiguchi Nyūdō, "but to spend long ages in the hells is indeed painful."

Then Takiguchi led him round to pray at all the monasteries and pagodas, coming at last to the Okuno-in, the tomb of Kōbō Daishi. Mount Kōya is two hundred ri from the Imperial Capital, silent and far from the habitations of men: untainted are the breezes that rustle its branches, calm are the shadows of its setting sun. Eight are its peaks and eight are its valleys, truly a place to purify the heart: beneath the forest mists the flowers blossom; the bells echo to the cloud-capped hills. On the tiles of its roofs the pine-shoots grow; mossy are its walls where the hoar-frost lingers.

In ancient times in the period Enki, in answer to a request in a dream from Kōbō Daishi, the Mikado Daigo Tennō sent a dark coloured robe to Kōya; but when the Imperial Messenger Chūnagon Sukezumi-no-Kyō ascended the mountain, accompanied by the Sōjō Kwangen of Hannyaji, and opened the doors of the holy tomb to put the new robe on the Daishi, a thick mist arose and hid his figure from their eyes. Bursting into tears Kwangen exclaimed: "Why are we not permitted to see him? This is the first time since I was born that I have received such a rebuke." And casting himself on the ground he wept bitterly. Then the mist gradually melted away, and the Daishi appeared like the moon from the clouds, and Kwangen, weeping now for joy, clothed him in the new garment and also shaved his hair which had grown very long.

Though the Imperial Messenger and the Sōjō Kwangen were able to see and adore the Daishi, the Sōjō's acolyte, Naigū Shunyū of Ishiyama, who had accompanied them, was unable to do so on account of his youth, and was greatly grieved in consequence, so the Sōjō took his hand and placed it upon the knee of the Daishi, and ever after this hand had a fragrant odour. It is said too that instruction for making incense of a similar scent is still handed down at the temple of Ishiyama. Now this was the reply that the Daishi sent to the Mikado: "In former days I met a Sattva, and from him learned all the secret tradition of Dharani and Mudra. In everlasting pity for the people of the world I took upon myself an unparalleled vow, and trusting in the great mercy of Fugen, exhibiting in myself perfect tranquillity in these far-off confines, I wait the coming of Maitreya." Not otherwise did Maha Kas'yapa retire to the cave in Mount Kukkrita to await the coming of universal peace. It was on the twenty-first day of the third month of the second year of Shōwa, at the Hour of the Tiger (4 a.m.), that Kōbō Daishi entered Nirvana, and that is now three hundred years ago, so that he has yet five billion six hundred and seventy million years to wait for the rebirth of Maitreya and the salvation of the world.

KOREMORI RENOUNCES THE WORLD

"I am forever undecided, like the birds on the snowy peaks of India that are always crying, 'to-day we will build our nest, or to-morrow;'" declared Koremori, weeping. Tanned by the salt breezes, and wasted by continual anxiety, he no longer looked like his former self, but even now he was far more comely than most men.

That night he returned to the cell of Takiguchi Nyūdō, and there they talked of many things both past and present. As the night grew on and he watched the deportment of the Nyūdō he perceived that he was indeed as it were polishing the jewel of Truth on the floor of profound faith, and at the boom of the bell at the Hour of the Tiger, he came to understand the unreality of this world of illusion. Early the next morning he called Chigaku Shōnin of Tozen-in and intimated to him that he wished to become a monk. He also summoned Yosōbyōye Shigekage and Ishidō Maru, and addressed them thus:

"As for me I am overwhelmed by unspeakable anxieties, and my way has become straitened so that I cannot escape, and whatever may become of me there is no need for you to throw away your lives. Many others are still living, so after I have met my fate, do you make haste to the Capital and help them, both cherishing my wife and children, and praying for my happier rebirth." On hearing this the two were for a while choked by emotion so that they could utter no word, but by and by Shigekage controlled his feelings and said: "At the time of the rebellion of Heiji my father Yosozaemon Kageyasu followed our lord Shigemori, and at Nijō Horikawa engaged Kamada Hyōye and fell by the hand of Akugenda. I also might have done some such deed, but at that time I was hardly two years old and so remember nothing of it. When I was seven years old my mother followed my father, and I was left alone with none to care for me, when your late father took compassion on me, saying that, as I was the son of one who had given his life for him, I should always be brought up in his house. And so I thought it natural to look forward to giving my life for yours some time or other, and it seems a great shame to me that you bid me run away and save myself in this fashion. Many may survive, as you say, but as things now are they will all be retainers of the Genji. And after you have departed this life, what pleasure can I have in living longer? And if one lived for a thousand, or ten thousand years, would not one have to die in the end? I can see no greater wisdom than this." And so saying he cut off his hair himself, and then received the tonsure from Takiguchi. When Ishidō Maru saw this, not to be outdone, he too cut off his hair. He had been with his master since he was eight years old, and his gratitude was no less than that of Shigekage, so he also had his head shaved by Takiguchi Nyūdō.

When Koremori saw what they had done he felt inexpressibly sad, and exclaimed: "Ah! I had thought to see my dear ones once again in my former state, but now I have nothing more to hope for." And so, as it must be, repeating three times the Buddhist text, "Whosoever is continuously reborn in the Three Worlds, it is because he cannot sever the bonds of affection. Whosoever renounces affection and enters Nirvana, he it is who in truth requites affection," he submitted his head to the tonsure. Both Koremori and Yosōbyōye were twenty-seven years old at this time, while Ishidō Maru was eighteen. By and by he called Takesato and said: "You are not to go up to the Capital now. In the end it can not be concealed, but if my wife were to know what I have done now, no doubt she too would renounce the world.

"But go to Yashima and tell them that, as they can see, the world is in a sad plight, and those who are tired of existence are many; perhaps they may not have heard that Hidan-no-Chūjō Kiyotsune fell in the Western Provinces, and Bitchū-no-kami Moromori was killed at Ichi-no-tani, while my chief regret is that they may think me recreant on account of my present behaviour. Moreover, as to this armour of Chinese leather, and the sword Kogarasu Maru, which have been handed down as heirlooms from Taira Sadamori, and have come to me after nine generations, in the event of fortune favouring our house again so that we are able to return to the Capital, you must take them and give them to my son Rokudai." Takesato, overcome by emotion, could make no reply for some time,

but after a while he restrained his feelings and said:
"Not till I have seen what is to befall will I leave my
master, but when all is ended I will go to Yashima."
Whereat Koremori allowed him to go with him. Then,
taking Takiguchi Nyūdō with them as a guide to salvation, they set out from Kōya in the guise of Yama-
bushi, and soon arrived at Santō in Kii.

THE PILGRIMAGE TO KUMANO

Thus proceeding on their way at length they came to
the Iwatagawa. And of this river it is said that whosoever crosses it is cleansed of all evil Karma and
hindrances to right conduct, and inherited sins. As he
offered up his prayers with a calm mind before the
Shōjōden of the main shrine, and throughout that night
contemplated the bulk of the stately temple, his heart
was filled with thoughts too deep for utterance. A
mist of boundless mercy and protection hovered over
the mountain of Yuya, and the matchless spiritual
power of the deity manifested itself in the Otonashi
River. The moon of the all-embracing efficacy of the
doctrine shone clear and without spot, and no dew of
evil thoughts collected in the garden of repentance for
the Six Roots of wickedness. Everything around
spoke to him of help and salvation.

As the night grew on and he meditated in the silence,
he pondered sadly over the remembrance of how his
father Shigemori had come to this shrine and entreated
the deity to shorten his days and grant him happiness
in the after life. And as the Buddha of this shrine is

Amida Nyorai, he prayed that, in accordance with his vow to save all mankind, he would bring him safe to the Pure Land, and also that his wife and children in Miyako might find peace and safety; for even when one has forsaken the world and entered the True Way, these blind attractions are not wholly absent.

The next day he took ship and went from the Hongū to the Shingū and worshipped the deity there. On its cliffs the pine-trees tower aloft; its breezes sweep all vain thoughts from the mind; while its clear flowing waters wash away the dust and mire of this evil world. Worshipping at the shrine of Asukai, and passing by Sano-no-Matsubara, he came to the shrine of Nachi. There is the famous threefold waterfall that soars up thousands of yards to the sky, where upon the top of the cliff there stands a figure of Kwannon, a spot that might be called Fudaraku-san: and as the sound of many voices chanting the Hokke Sutra came out of the mist it might be considered like the peak of Gridhrakuta. So since the time that the Buddha became reincarnate in this mountain all the people of our country from highest to lowest have come on pilgrimage to bow their heads and pray at this shrine, and therefrom have received great benefits. Hence are the temple roofs so many, and the courts crowded with priests and laymen. In the summer season of the period of Kwan-wa the Hō-ō Kwazan, an Emperor possessing the Ten Virtues, came to pray for rebirth in the heaven of Amida, and on the site of the cell where he stayed an ancient cherry-tree in bloom still recalls his memory.

KOREMORI DROWNS HIMSELF

So Koremori, after completing the pilgrimage to the three shrines of Kumano, took a boat before the shrine called Hama-no-miya, and launched out to the open sea. There is an island far out in the offing called Yamanari-no-shima, and to this he rowed and disembarked on the shore. Weeping bitterly he cut his name and pedigree on a great pine-tree thus: "Sammi-no-Chūjō Koremori, religious name Jō-en, son of Komatsu-no-Naidaijin Shigemori Kō, religious name Jō-ren, grandson of the Dajō-daijin Taira-no-Ason Kiyomori, religious name Jō-kai, aged twenty-seven years; drowns himself in the offing of Nachi, twenty-eighth day of the third month of the third year of Ju-ei;" after which he again entered the boat and rowed out into the offing.

Though he had made up his mind to end his life, when it came to the point he felt downcast and sad. As it was the twenty-eighth day of the third month a sea-mist was rolling over the waters, wrapping everything in a dreary pall; but even on an ordinary spring day a melancholy mood comes over us with the approach of evening, so how much more when to-day is the end, the last evening we spend on earth. Looking at the fishing-boats as they rose and sank on the waves, though he had made up his mind to sink likewise, yet his thoughts dwelt on his own fate, and when he saw a flock of wild-geese he felt as great regret and home-sickness for his birthplace as did Su Wu when he was imprisoned in the land of the Hsiung Nu, and sent

back a message by a wild-goose. Recollecting himself,
however, and reproving himself for harbouring such
vain thoughts of this world, he put his hands together,
and turning to the west repeated the Nembutsu. But
even so the thought came into his mind how his dear
ones in Miyako did not know that this was his last
hour, and would keep on waiting and hoping for some
tidings of him, so dropping his hands and ceasing to
say the Nembutsu, he turned to Takiguchi Nyūdō and
said: "Ah, what a thing it is to have wife and children!
For not only are they an anxiety in this world, but a
hindrance to obtaining Enlightenment in the next. I
fear that the obtrusion of these thoughts is because of
the greatness of my guilt, and I repent of it."

The sage felt deeply grieved in his heart, but thinking it would not do to show any weakness, he wiped
away his tears and assumed an impassive expression.
"Alas!" he said, "tender feelings are common to all
men, and it is indeed as you say. Endless are the
karma-relations produced if a man and woman place
their pillows together but for one night, and deep is
the connexion in their after lives. 'Those that are
born must die; those that meet must part,' is the way
of this world. 'The last dew or the first drop,' one
must go before the other, and whether one die soon or
late, all must leave this world at last. The pledge of
Hsuan Tsung to Yang Kuei Fei on an evening in
autumn at the Li Sang Palace led but to the bruising
of hearts, and even the love of the Emperor Wu
for the Lady Li had to come to an end. Even the
magicians Sung Tz' and Mei Sheng did not live for

ever, neither are the highest rank of saints free from
birth and death; so that even if you can boast of the
pleasures of long life, this regret cannot be put away.
Thus if you live for a hundred years, the pain of parting will still be the same. And Mara the king of evil
in the sixth Devaloka, who opposes the Way, taking
possession of the Six Heavens of Desire, has made
them his own, and grudging the people of these worlds
deliverance from birth and death, becomes to them
wives and husbands to hinder their escape; and so all
the Buddhas of the Three Worlds, regarding all mankind as their children, in their zeal to bring them to the
Paradise of the Pure Land, have strictly warned them
that from the utmost antiquity wives and children were
fetters to bind them to the Wheel of Birth and Death.
But Amida Nyorai, the Buddha of this shrine, has
made forty-eight vows to save mankind, and among
these in the eighteenth vow he states that whosoever in
true faith shall call up to ten times on his name,
earnestly desiring to enter Paradise, shall in no wise
fail to attain Enlightenment. So if indeed you believe
this doctrine, relying on it in firm faith without any
doubt, and if you repeat the Nembutsu either once or
ten times, Amida Nyorai, diminishing to some sixteen
feet his august stature, which is of a height that
myriads of Nahutas, many in number as the sands of
the Ganges, only can measure, with Kwannon and
Seishi and innumerable Saints and Bodhisattvas en-
compassing them about tier on tier, will come forth to
meet you from the Eastern Gate of Paradise, welcom-
ing your advent with songs of rejoicing.

"Thus though your body may sink to the bottom of this ocean, you will ride in glory on clouds of purple. And when you have become a Buddha and attained liberation, in true Enlightenment you may come back to this world, and without doubt may lead your wife and child into the path of true salvation." And as he spoke thus, striking his bell the while, and urging him to repeat the Nembutsu, Koremori, in sure belief that he had attained Enlightenment, steadfastly putting aside all vain thoughts, looked towards the west and clasped his hands, with a loud voice repeating the Nembutsu a hundred times, and then with the word "Namu" on his lips sprang into the ocean. Yasōbyōye and Ishidō Maru, repeating the same invocation, also sprang to their death with their master.

Now after the Heike had crossed over to Yashima, they heard that a force of many tens of thousands of horsemen had arrived at the Capital from the East Country to advance against them, and moreover that the parties of Usuki, Hetsuki and Matsuura had banded together and were about to cross from Kyūshū to attack them. And as these various rumours came to their ears they could not help being dispirited and discouraged; and all the Court Ladies, from the Consort of the late Emperor, Kenrei-mon-in, the Mother of the late Emperor, and the Nii Dono downwards mourned and lamented together, wondering what fresh evil tidings they would have to hear, or what new adversities they would have to meet. And seeing that so many of the Nobles had been killed and more than half of the best of the retainers also lost at Ichi-no-

tani, Awa-no-Mimbu Shigeyoshi and his brother and
the other men of Shikoku remarked how their
strength had lessened, but still they thought they would
be safe trusting to the mountains and the sea. On the
twenty-fifth day of the seventh month the ladies came
together saying that it was just a year since they had
left Miyako, and wondering how soon the time had
passed; and so, bewailing the vicissitudes they had met,
and talking of reminiscences of the past, some gave
way to tears and some to laughter.

It was now autumn, and the wind began to blow in
the stalks of the lespedeza, while the dew hung heavy
on its lower leaves. The resentful hum of the insects,
the rustling of the rice-stalks and the falling of the
leaves, all bring sad thoughts, and the quickly darken-
ing skies of the short days of autumn always cause
gloomy feelings, so we can well imagine how much
more melancholy must those of the Heike have been.
In former days they used to divert themselves with the
spring flowers in the Palace gardens, but now they
languished under the autumn moon by the shore of
Yashima. While they composed verses to the bright
moon, the evenings of Miyako were ever in their
thoughts, and so they consoled themselves with tears
in their eyes. The following verse made by Sama-no-
kami Yukimori well expresses their feelings:

> Where our Sovereign dwells
> Like the moon above the clouds,
> There must be our Court;
> But the ancient Capital
> Still is nearest to our hearts.

Now if the Commander-in-chief Noriyori had continued to prosecute his attack on the Heike, he could have easily destroyed them, but instead of that he remained with his army at Murotsu and Takasago, amusing himself with a lot of courtesans and harlots that he had got together, and wasting the resources of the country as well as troubling the people to no small extent; and though there were many lords of the East Country with him, both great and small, as he was in supreme command they could do nothing. And in this way the year ended.

Yoshitsune Crosses to Yashima

Now on the third day of the second month Kurō Hōgwan Yoshitsune started from Miyako and proceeded to Watanabe and Fukushima in Settsu to get his ships in order, with the intention of attacking Yashima immediately. On the same day his brother Mikawa-no-kami Noriyori left the Capital also, and he too went to Kanzaki in Settsu to prepare his ships for a campaign against the Sanyodo. On the tenth day of the same month the Hō-ō sent an Imperial Envoy to the shrines of Ise and Iwashimizu, and gave orders that all the chief priests of all shrines should offer up prayers for the speedy return of the Emperor and the Three Sacred Treasures to the Capital.

On the sixteenth day, just as the ships that had been prepared at Watanabe and Fukushima were about to loose their hawsers and set sail, a most violent tempest arose, and the ships were damaged so that they could not put out, so that day was spent in repairing them.

Then the leaders of the Eastern Provinces, great and small, came together at Watanabe and said: "We have so far had no experience of war at sea, so what shall we do?" "I think we ought to have a 'Sakaro' fitted on these ships," put in Kajiwara. "A 'Sakaro?' What is that?" asked Yoshitsune. "When you ride a horse," replied Kajiwara, "you can gallop forward or back at your pleasure, because it is quite easy to turn either to the right or the left, but it is a pretty difficult matter to swing a ship round; so if we fit oars at both bow and stern, instead of only at the stern as usual, and insert a rudder in the middle, then we shall be able to turn about easily just as we like."

"What an ill-omened thing to propose at the beginning of a campaign," exclaimed Yoshitsune, "you know armies always set out with the intention of never retreating, and it is only if they meet with a disaster that they retire, so what is the meaning of these preparations for running away? You lords may fit a hundred or a thousand pairs of 'backing-oars' or 'turn-back-oars' or whatever you like to call them, to your ships, but I shall go with no more than the usual number."

"A good general," returned Kajiwara, "is one who advances at the proper time, and retreats at the proper time, thus saving his own life and destroying the enemy; that is what is called a good general: but a man of only one idea is called a 'wild-boar-warrior,' and is not thought much of." "Wild-boar or stag, it's all one; the best way to conquer in battle is to attack the enemy's front, and attack again and again."

Then the chiefs of the Eastern Provinces, as they did not dare to laugh openly at Kajiwara, showed their feelings in their features, and muttered under their breath to each other. Yoshitsune and Kajiwara were on the point of drawing their weapons on each other that day, but fortunately the incident was concluded without any actual quarrel. "Now the ships are repaired and ready," said Yoshitsune, "let us have a bite and a cup in celebration;" and while this was being done the stores and weapons and horses were got on board, and all being prepared he gave the order to set sail. The captains and crews murmured at this, however, crying out: "We have the wind behind us, it is true, but it is a little too strong, and the sea will be very rough outside."

This angered Yoshitsune exceedingly. "Do you think I am going to stop putting to sea for a little wind?" he cried. "Whether you die on the sea or on land, it is all the result of the Karma of a former life; and if I told you to put out in the teeth of a head-wind you might blame me with some reason, but with the wind behind us, even if it is a little fresher than usual, not to put out at a critical time like this . . . ! Ho! Men-at-arms! Shoot these fellows if they won't move!" Then Ise Saburō Yoshimori, Satō Saburō Tsuginobu and Sato Shirōhyōye Tadanobu of Mutsu, Eda-no-Genzō, Kumai-no-Tarō, Musashi-bō Benkei and others, each equal to a thousand ordinary men, at once sprang forth. "At our lord's command!" they shouted, "Off with those ships, or we shoot every one of you!" So when the captains and sailors saw them running up with their bows in their hands they cried out: "Whether we drown out there in the sea or are shot here, it is all the same, so put off!"

And so of the two hundred odd ships five at last got away. These five were, first the Hōgwan's ship; then Tajiro-no-Kwanja's ship; then that of Gotōbyōye and his son; then that of the brothers Kaneko, and that of Yodo-no-Gonai Tadatoshi, who held the office of Funa-bugyo, or Marshal of the Ships. The rest of the ships, whether from fear of Kajiwara or the weather, did not put out.

"There's no need to stop for the others," said Yoshitsune, "at ordinary times the enemy would be afraid and on the alert, but on a stormy day like this we can land at a place where he won't be expecting us; thus we can attack him to advantage. And take care to cover your lights. If the enemy sees many lights he will take alarm. Follow my ship by keeping your eye on my head and stern lights." So they sailed on all night, and in six hours covered a distance that usually took three days. It was about two o'clock in the morning on the sixteenth day of the second month that they set sail from Watanabe and Fukushima in Settsu, and they arrived off the coast of Awa the next morning about seven.

THE CROSSING OF OSAKA

Yoshitsune next asked Kondō Roku how many men the Heike had at Yashima, to which he replied that the number was not more than a thousand horsemen.

"How is it that there are so few?" said the Hōgwan. "Because they have stationed bands of fifty or a hundred men at every creek and island round Shikoku, and also because an army of three thousand horse under the command of Dennai Saemon Noriyoshi, the eldest son of Awa-no-Mimbu Shigeyoshi, has gone over to Iyo to attack Kōno Shirō of that province, because he would not join them when they summoned him."

"Ah, that's a fine opportunity! I have them. And how far is it to Yashima from here?" "About two days march," replied Kondō. "Then let us hurry up and get there before they get wind of us." And so they started off, sometimes running and sometimes marching, making as great a speed as they could, until by night they came to the mountain pass of Osaka on the borders of Awa and Sanuki, and began to cross it.

About the middle of the night as they were pushing on over the mountain, they came up with a man carrying a letter. As it was dark he had not the least idea that they were enemies, but thought they were Heike soldiers going to Yashima, and began to talk to them quite freely. "You seem to be going to Yashima, so I suppose you know the way," said Yoshitsune. "Can you guide us?" "Certainly," replied the man, "I often go there, so I know the road very well." "Who is that letter from, and who is it for?" asked Yoshitsune. "It is from the Ladies in Miyako, and I am taking it to the Daijin Munemori in Yashima," was the reply. "What is it about?" "The Genji have already got as far as Yodo and Kawajiri, so no doubt it is to send him tidings of it." "Ah, no doubt `that is so," exclaimed the Hōgwan, "seize that letter, men! But don't kill him," he added as they took the letter, "for that would be a useless crime."

So they bound the man to a tree in the mountains and passed on. When Yoshitsune opened the letter and read it, he found that it was indeed from the Ladies in Miyako. "Kurō is a shrewd fellow," he read, "and will not fear to attack however rough the weather may be, so take care not to scatter your force, and be very much on the alert." "This letter is godsend to me," said Yoshitsune, "we must keep it and show it to Yoritomo." And he stowed it away very carefully.

Now at Yashima Dennai Saemon Noriyoshi, the eldest son of Awa-no-Mimbu Shigeyoshi, had ridden into the province of Iyo with three thousand horse to chastise Konō-no-Shirō for not coming to join them when he was summoned, but Konō himself had escaped him, so he cut off the heads of some hundred and fifty of his retainers and marched back with them to the Palace. But as he thought it was not proper to bring the heads of rebels to the Palace for inspection, he took them to the headquarters of Munemori, when suddenly his men began to shout out that the houses of Takamatsu were on fire. "As it is daytime it is not likely to be accidental," he cried. "It must be the enemy who is here and has set them on fire. They are sure to be in great force, so we can do nothing. Come! Come! Into the boats!" And in great hurry and confusion they scrambled aboard the ships that were

moored in rows along the beach in front of the main
gate.

In the Imperial Ship were the Imperial Consort
Kenrei-mon-in, the mother of the late Emperor and the
Nii Dono* with their Ladies-in-waiting, while Munemori was in another with his son, and the others got on
board any ship they could find, and all the ships immediately rowed out a cho or thirty or forty yards from
the shore. Scarcely had they done so when the seventy
or eighty horsemen of the Genji, all armed alike, galloped smartly up to the beach in front of the main gate.

As the tide was at its lowest ebb in the tidal bay, the
water came up to the horses' chests, or knees, or girths
in some places, and in others it was shallower still,
and so as they dashed through the waves, kicking up a
mist of foam and spray all round them, out of which
their white banners appeared fluttering here and there,
it was no wonder that the Heike, doomed as they were,
should imagine that a great army was upon them.
Especially was this so in that Yoshitsune, not wishing
that the enemy should see the smallness of his force,
had divided it up into small groups of from five to
ten horsemen each.

He was attired that day in a hitatare of red, and
armour of shaded purple, and wore a helmet surmounted by golden horns, a gold-mounted sword, and a
quiver of black and white feathered arrows, twenty-
four in number. Grasping his rattan-bound bow in the
middle he glared fiercely at the enemy out in the offing,

*The nun of the Second Court Rank. Wife of Kiyomori.

and shouted with a loud voice: "I am Minamoto Yoshitsune, Lord High Constable, Envoy of the Hō-ō." After him the rest of the leaders of the Genji proclaimed their names and titles. As they came riding up, shouting their war-cries, the Heike seized their bows and began to shoot from far and near, but the Genji took but little heed of them, ducking to left and right to avoid the shafts, and taking the opportunity to rest and breathe their horses under the lee of those ships that were in shallow water, all the while shouting and fighting furiously.

THE DEATH OF TSUGINOBU

Now Gotōbyōye Sanemoto, a veteran warrior, did not stop to take part in the fight on the beach, but went on and burst into the Palace and set it on fire, so that it went up in flames in a moment. The Daijin Munemori, seeing this, turned to his retainers and inquired: "How many men have the Genji?" "Not more than seventy or eighty horsemen, it seems," was the reply. "Ah, so few?" exclaimed Munemori; "if the hair of their heads was counted one by one, they would not equal our force! Why did you lose your heads and run away to the ships, and let them through without a blow to set fire to the Palace? Is not Noritsune here? Let him land and give battle to these fellows!"

At this order Noto-no-kami Noritsune landed with some five hundred men in small boats, under the command of Etchū-no-Jirōhyōye Moritsugu, and took up a position on the beach in front of the burnt-out main gate. Yoshitsune also drew up his eighty horsemen opposite them, about a bowshot away. Then Etchū-no-Jirōhyōye came forth on to the deck-house of his boat and shouted in a loud voice: "Ho, there! You may perhaps have declared your name and titles once already, but as it was far away over the sea, we could not hear. So who is the leader of the Genji with whom we have to do to-day?" "It is needless to repeat it," shouted Ise Saburō in reply, "but here is the Lord Yoshitsune, the younger brother of Yoritomo, lord of Kamakura, descended in the tenth generation from the Emperor Seiwa!"

"Oh!" retorted Moritsugu, "then that is the wretched little stripling, who was left an orphan when his father was killed in the Heiji fighting, and who became an acolyte at Kurama temple, and ran away to Mutsu carrying baggage in the train of a gold merchant."

"Why show off your eloquence in such talk about our lord," replied Yoshimori, drawing nearer, "I fancy you are one of those who got yourself well beaten at Tonamiyama in the north, and just escaped with your life, to beg your way home all the way from the Hokurikudo, aren't you?"

"What need to be a beggar when one has a bounteous lord to depend on?" said Moritsugu, "I didn't get my living and keep my family on robbing and thieving in Suzugayama in Ise, and being a low retainer, as you did." At this point Kaneko-no-Jūrō came forward and interrupted them. "What's the good of all this useless talk? Calling one another names is a thing anyone can do. These lords know what our young warriors

of Musashi and Sagami can do from what they saw at
Ichi-no-tani last spring."

And as he spoke his younger brother, who had so
far stood by his side without a word, took an arrow
twelve handbreadths and three fingers long, fitted it to
his bow and drew with all his might, so that the arrow
flew straight at Moritsugu and stuck in his breastplate
with such force as to pierce it right through, thus
putting an end to the wordy warfare.

Now Noto-no-kami Noritsune was attired as for a
sea-fight without hitatare and full armour, but in a
short under-robe dyed in variegated colours, and
armour laced with Chinese silk. His sword was
mounted in gold and silver, and he carried a "Shigeto"
bow and a quiver of twenty-four arrows feathered
with hawk's tail-feathers. He was the most redoubtable archer in the Imperial Camp and it was said of
him that he never missed anyone he aimed at.

With the intention of putting an end to Yoshitsune
at a single shot he stood watching his mark, but the
Genji perceived this, and Ise Saburō, Satō Saburōhyōye
Tsuginobu, Satō Shirōhyōye Tadanobu, Eda-no-Genzō,
Kumai Tarō and Musashi-bō Benkei rode up in a line
close together in front of Yoshitsune to protect him
from the arrows, so that it was impossible for Noto-
no-kami to hit him. "Get out of the way of the arrows,
you fellows!" he shouted, and drawing his bow again
and again with great speed and accuracy he shot down
ten of the Genji soldiers, among whom Satō Saburōhyōye, who was in the forefront, received an arrow that
pierced him through from the left shoulder to the right

armpit, and no longer able to sit his horse, fell head-long to the ground.

Then one of Noto-no-kami's young men named Kikuō Maru, a very strong fighter, wearing a body armour of green colour and a helmet of three plates, drew his sword and ran out to take the head of Tsuginobu. At this his younger brother Tadanobu, who was standing beside him, drew his bow and shot Kikuō Maru under the skirts of his armour, so that he sank down on to his knees.

When Noritsune saw this, still holding his bow in his left hand, with his right he seized Kikuō Maru and flung him back into his own ship. Thus he prevented the Genji from taking his head, though he died later from the wound.

Then Yoshitsune, ordering them to carry Tsuginobu to the rear, sprang down from his horse and took him by the hand, saying: "How do you feel, Saburōhyōye?" "It is the end, my lord," answered Tsuginobu. "Is there anything you would wish for in this world?" inquired Yoshitsune. "What is there that I should want? Only that I regret that I shall not live to see my lord come to his own. For the rest, it is the destiny of one who wields the bow and arrow to fall by the shaft of an enemy. And that it should be told to future genera-tions that I, Satō Saburōhyōye Tsuginobu of Mutsu, died instead of my lord at the fight on the beach of Yashima in Sanuki, in the war of the Genji and Heike, will be my pride in this life and something to remember on the dark road of death." And so he died.

Stout warrior as Yoshitsune was, he was so overcome

with grief that he pressed the sleeve of his armour to his face and wept bitterly. He then asked if there was any reverend priest in those parts, and when they had found one he said: "A wounded man has just died; I wish you to recite the Sutras for him for one day," and he presented him with a stout black horse with a fine set of trappings.

This was the horse that Yoshitsune, when he received the Fifth Rank, also raised to the Fifth Rank and gave the name of Taiyū Kurō. It was the one on which he had descended the Hiyodorigoe pass behind Ichi-no-tani. When the other samurai, and especially Tsuginobu's younger brother Tadanobu, saw this, they were moved to tears and exclaimed: "For the sake of a lord like this, who would consider his life more than dust or dew?"

NASU-NO-YŌICHI

Now as those warriors of Awa and Sanuki who wished to throw off their allegiance to the Heike and join the Genji began to emerge from their caves and mountains in small bands of fifteen and twenty, and ride in to join him, Yoshitsune soon found himself in command of a force of some three hundred horse.

By this time the sun was sinking and both armies were preparing to retire, as no decision could be reached that day, when from the offing a small boat, with no special decoration, was seen to come rowing to the shore. When it had reached a distance of seven or eight "tan" from the water's edge, it swung round broadside on, and while the Heike wondered what it would do, a girl, some eighteen or nineteen years old, wearing a five-fold robe of white lined with green, and a scarlet hakama, took a red fan with a rising sun on it and hung it up on a pole fastened to the gunwhale of the boat.

Calling Gotōbyōye Sanemoto, Yoshitsune asked him what was the meaning of it. "It is to shoot at, no doubt," replied Gotō, "I expect it is a plan of theirs to get you to come and look at this charmer, and entice you out in front into bowshot, but at any rate we ought to shoot it away." "Who is the best archer we have?" asked Yoshitsune. "There are several good shots, but the best is Yōichi Munetaka, the son of Nasu-no-Tarō Suketaka of Shimozuke. He is a small man, but a most skilful archer." "What proof have you?" asked Yoshitsune. "He can hit two or three birds on the wing with anybody." "Then call him," was the reply.

Yōichi was then barely twenty years old. He was wearing a hitatare of greenish blue with the collar and edges of the sleeves ornamented with brocade on a red ground. His armour was laced with light green and the mounts of his sword were of silver. He carried twenty-four arrows with black and white feathers, or rather dark-grey, in which hawks' wing-feathers were mixed. A turnip-headed arrow pointed with staghorn was also stuck in his quiver. Carrying his Shigeto bow under his arm, and with his helmet slung to his breast-plate, he came into the presence of the Hōgwan and did obeisance.

"How now, Yōichi," said Yoshitsune, "can you hit

that fan right in the middle, and show the enemy how we can shoot?" "I cannot say for certain," replied Yōichi, "and if I should miss, it would be a lasting reproach to the skill of our side. So it would be better to entrust it to some one who could be quite sure."

This reply greatly angered Yoshitsune. "Those who came from Kamakura with me on this campaign must obey my orders," he exclaimed, "those who do not had better go back there again!" Then Yōichi, thinking it would not do to refuse again, replied: "I may not succeed in hitting it, but as my lord commands, I will try." And retiring he mounted a fine black horse with saddle ornamented with gold, and taking a fresh hold on his bow, he gripped the reins and rode into the sea. Those on his own side, looking after him, exclaimed: "Ah, that young fellow is sure to bring it down!" And the Hōgwan also thought he had not misplaced his trust.

As it was a little beyond bowshot he rode about one tan into the water, but still the fan seemed about seven tan* away. It was the eighteenth day of the second month, and the Hour of the Cock (6 p.m.). The wind was blowing rather strongly from the north, and the waves were running high on the beach. Out in the offing the ships were rising and falling as they rode

---

*A tan is said to be usually 60 ken (1 ken=6 feet) so it would be about 450 feet, which the commentator considers too far. In these ancient war chronicles a tan is reckoned as one jo or 10 feet, but this is too little. But to hit the rivet of a fan at 70 feet would not be easy and the shorter distance seems more likely.

on the swell, and the fan was fluttering about in the breeze. The Heike had ranged their ships in a long line to see better what would befall, while on land the Genji lined the shore in expectation. The whole of both armies were watching the scene.

Then Yōichi closed his eyes and prayed: "Hachiman Dai-bosatsu, God of Battles, and ye deities of my homeland, the Gongen of Nikko, Yuzen Daimyōjin of Nasu of Utsunomiya, I pray you grant that I may strike the centre of that fan. For if I fail, I will break my bow and put an end to my life, showing my face no more among men. If therefore you will that I see home again, let not this arrow miss its mark." After praying thus silently he again opened his eyes, and the wind had abated a little so that the fan looked easier to hit.

Taking the turnip-headed shaft he drew his bow with all his strength and let fly. He was short of stature, it is true, but his arrow measured twelve hand-breadths and three fingers, and his bow was a strong one. The shore echoed to the whirr of the arrow as it flew straight to its mark. Whizzing it struck the fan an inch from the rivet, so that it flew up into the air as the arrow fell into the sea. Once and again the spring breeze caught it and tossed it up, then suddenly it dropped down into the water. And when they saw the scarlet fan gleaming in the rays of the setting sun as it danced up and down, rising and falling on the white crests of the waves, the Heike in the offing beat applaudingly on the gunwales of their ships, while the

Genji on the shore rattled their quivers till they rang again.

THE DROPPED BOW

Unable to restrain himself in his excitement over the enjoyment of this feat, an old warrior of some fifty years of age, in armour laced with black leather, sprang up on one of the ships just in the place where the fan had been and began to dance, twirling a white-handled halberd in his hand.

Seeing this, Ise Saburō Yoshimori came up behind Yōichi and said: "It is our lord's command that you bring down that fellow too." So Yōichi took one of the middle arrows of his quiver, drew his bow and let fly. The arrow flew straight to the mark, hitting the dancer right in the middle of his body so that he fell back into the bottom of the boat. There were some who applauded this shot also, but most showed their disapproval by shouting: "Too bad! Too bad! That was a cruel thing to do." Silence now ensued on the side of the Heike, though the Genji still continued to rattle their quivers.

Then from the Heike side, still disinclined to rest under their discomfiture, there came three warriors, one armed with a bow, the second carrying a shield, and the third a halberd. Springing on shore they dared the Genji to come on, whereat Yoshitsune called out to know who of the younger of his best horsemen would try conclusions with these insolent fellows.

Then there rode forth Mionoya Jūrō of Musashi,

and his two brothers Shirō and Tōshichi, Nibu-no-Shirō of Kōzuke and Kiso-no-Chūji of Shinano, five warriors in all. As they charged forward shouting to the onset, however, the archer behind the shield loosed a great lacquered shaft, feathered with black wing-feathers, which pierced the horse of Mionoya Jūrō in the left breast right up to the notch, so that it collapsed like an overturned screen.

The rider at once threw his left leg over the animal and vaulted down to the right, drawing his sword to continue the fight, but when he saw the warrior behind the shield come to meet him flourishing a huge halberd, he knew that his own small sword would be useless, and blew on a conch and retreated. The other immediately followed him, and it looked as though he would cut him down with the halberd, but instead of doing so, gripping the halberd under his left arm, he tried to seize Mionoya Jūrō by the neckpiece of the helmet with his right.

Three times Mionoya eluded his grasp, but at the fourth attempt his opponent held on. For a moment he could do nothing, but then, giving a sudden violent wrench, the neckpiece parted where it joined the helmet, and Mionoya escaped and hid behind his four companions to recover his breath. The other four, wishing to spare their horses, had taken no part in the combat, but stayed a short way off looking on. The Heike warrior on his part did not follow him any farther, but sticking the neckpiece on the end of his halberd, shouted out in a loud voice: "Let those afar off listen; those who are near can see. That's the way we fellows of the Capital declare ourselves. I am Aku-shichibyōye Kagekiyo of Kazusa!" And having thus delivered himself he retired again behind the shield.

The Heike, encouraged at this, cried out: "Don't let Aku-shichibyōye be killed! To the rescue of Kagekiyo! Come on, men!" And some two hundred of them hastened to land and set up their shields in a row in hen's wing style, defying the Genji to come on. Yoshitsune, incensed at this, with Tajiro-no-Kwanja in front, Ise Saburō behind, and Gotōbyōye father and son and the brothers Kaneko on his left and right hand, put himself at the head of eighty horsemen and charged down on them shouting, whereupon the Heike, who were mostly on foot and few mounted, thinking they could not stand against horsemen, quickly retired and re-entered their boats, leaving their shields kicked about here and there like the sticks of a fortune-teller.

Elated with victory, the Genji rode into the sea in pursuit till they were up to their saddles in water and fought among the ships, while the Heike with rakes and billhooks tried to seize Yoshitsune by the neck-piece of his helmet. Two or three times their weapons rattled about his head, but his companions with sword and halberd warded off the attacks from their master as they fought. In the course of this fighting he somehow or other dropped his bow into the sea, and leant out of the saddle trying to pick it up again with his whip. His companions cried out to him to let it go, but he would not, and at last managed to recover it, and rode back laughing to the beach.

The older warriors reproached him for this saying: "However valuable a bow it might be, what is that in comparison with our lord's life?" "It was not that I grudged the bow," replied Yoshitsune, "and if my bow were one that required two or three men to bend it, like that of my uncle Tametomo, they would be quite welcome to it, but I should not like a weak one like mine to fall into the hands of the enemy for them to laugh at it and say, 'This is the bow of Kurō Yoshitsune the Commander-in-Chief of the Genji;' and so it was that I risked my life to get it back." And this explanation drew expressions of approval from all.

THE COCK-FIGHT BEFORE THE DEITY

Meanwhile Yoshitsune, after his victory at Yashima, crossed over to Suwo to join his brother Noriyori, and, strange to say, the place which the Heike next reached was called Hikushima in the province of Nagato, while the Genji went to Oitsu in the same province. Just at this time Tansō, the Lord Steward of Kumano, of the province of Kii, who was under great obligations to the Heike, suddenly changed his mind and hesitated as to which side he should support. So he went to the shrine of Ikumano at Tanabe and spent seven days in retirement there, having Kagura performed, and praying before the Gongen. As a result of this he received an intimation from the deity that he should adhere to the white banner, but, being still doubtful, he took seven white cocks and seven red ones, and held a cock-fight before the Gongen, and as none of the red cocks were victorious but were all beaten and ran away, he at last made up his mind to join the Genji. Therefore, assembling all his retainers to the number of some two thousand men, and embarking them on two hundred ships of war, he put the emblem of the deity of the shrine on board his ship and painted the name of Kongo Dōji on the top of his standard. Accordingly when this vessel with its divine burden approached the ships of the Genji and Heike at Dan-no-ura, both parties saluted it reverently, but when it was seen to direct its course towards the fleet of the Genji, the Heike could not conceal their chagrin. Moreover, to the further consternation of the Heike, Kono-no-Shiro Michinobu of the province of Iyo also came rowing up with a hundred and fifty large ships and went over to the fleet of their enemies.

Thus the forces of the Genji went on increasing, while those of the Heike grew less. The Genji had some three thousand ships, and the Heike one thousand, among which were some of Chinese build; and so, on the twenty-fourth day of the third month of the second year of Gen-ryaku, at the Hour of the Hare (6 a.m.), at Ta-no-ura in the province of Bungo, at Moji-ga-seki, and at Dan-no-ura in the province of Nagato, at Akamagaseki, began the final battle of the Gen and Hei.

THE FIGHT AT DAN-NO-URA

Now the two hosts of the Genji and Heike faced each other scarcely thirty cho distant on the water; and as the tide was running strongly through Moji, Akama and Dan-no-ura, the Heike ships were carried down by the current against their will, while the Genji were naturally able to advance on them with the tide. Kaji-wara with his sons and retainers to the number of fourteen or fifteen, stuck close to the shore, and catching on with rakes to some ships of the Heike that went astray, they boarded them and sprang from one ship to the other, cutting their men down both at bow and stern and doing great deeds. And their merit that day has been specially recorded.

Thus both armies joined battle all along the line, and the roar of their war-cries was such as to be heard even to the highest heavens of Brahma, and to cause the deity deep under the earth to start in amazement. Then Tomomori, coming forth on to the deck-house of his ship, shouted to his men in a mighty voice: "Even in India and China and also in our own country, with the most renowned leader and the bravest warriors an army cannot prevail if fate be against it. Yet must our honour be dear to us, and we must show a bold front to these Eastern soldiers. Let us then pay no heed to our lives, but think of nothing but fighting as bravely as we may." Hida-no-Saburō Saemon Kaget-sune again repeated this proclamation to the samurai. "Ho! these Eastern fellows may have a great name for their horsemanship," shouted Aku-shichibyōye Kage-kiyo, "but they know nothing about sea-fights, and they will be like fish up a tree, so that we will pick them up one by one and pitch them into the sea!" "And let their Commander Kurō Yoshitsune be the special object of your attack," added Etchū-no-Jirōhyōye

Moritsugu, "he is a little fellow with a fair complexion and his front teeth stick out a bit, so you will know him by that. He often changes his clothes and armour, so take care he doesn't escape you!" "Who cares for that wretched little fellow?" replied Aku-shichi, "Cheer up, my brave comrades; we'll soon pick him up under our arms and fling him into the sea!"

After Shin-Chūnagon Tomomori had thus addressed his men he took a small boat and rowed across to the ship of Munemori. "Our own men look well enough," said he, "only Awa-no-Mimbu Shigeyoshi seems doubtful in his allegiance. I pray you let me take off his head." "But he has served us well so far," replied Munemori, "so how can we do this only on suspicion? Anyhow, let him be summoned."

So Shigeyoshi came into the presence of Munemori. He was attired in a hitatare of yellowish red colour with a little black in it, and armour laced with light red leather. "How now, Shigeyoshi? Do you intend treachery?" said Munemori, "for your conduct to-day has a suspicious look. Do you tell your men of Shi-koku to bear themselves well in the fight, and don't play the dastard." "Why should I play the dastard?" said Shigeyoshi as he retired. Meanwhile Tomomori had been standing by with his hand gripping his sword-hilt hard enough to break it, casting meaning looks at Munemori to intimate his wish to cut Shigeyoshi down, but as the latter gave no sign he could do nothing.

So the Heike divided their thousand vessels into three fleets. In the van rowed Yamaga-no-Hyōtōji Hidetō with five hundred ships, and after him came the

Matsuura with three hundred more; last of all came the Heike nobles with two hundred. Now Yamaga-no-Hyōtōji who led the van was the strongest archer in all Kyūshū, and he chose five hundred men who drew the bow better than most, though not equal to himself, and placed them in the bows of his ships, shoulder to shoulder, so that they let fly a volley of five hundred arrows at once.

The fleet of the Genji was the more numerous with its three thousand ships, but as their men shot from various places here and there, their force did not show to advantage. Yoshitsune himself, who was fighting in the forefront of the battle, was greatly embarrassed by the arrows of the foe that fell like rain on his shield and armour. So, elated by their victory in the first attack, the Heike pressed onward, and the roar of their shouting mingled with the booming of their war-drums that continuously sounded the onset.

Now on the side of the Genji, Wada-no-Kōtarō Yoshimori did not go on shipboard, but mounted his horse and sat himself firmly in the saddle with his feet deep in the stirrups, riding into the midst of the Heike host and letting fly his arrows right and left. A famous archer he had always been, and no enemy within the space of three cho escaped his arrows, but one shaft he shot an extraordinary distance on which was a request to return it to the marksman. When it was withdrawn by order of Tomomori it was seen to be feathered with white wing-feathers of the crane mixed with black ones of the wild-goose, a plain bamboo shaft thirteen handbreadths and three fingers long, inscribed

at the space of a handbreath from the lashing on the
butt with the name Wada-no-Kōtarō Yoshimori
painted in lacquer.

Among the Heike too there were some fine archers,
but none who could do a feat like this. After a while
however, Nii-no-Kishirō Chikakiyo of Iyo stepped forward and shot it back again. It flew to a distance of
more than three cho and struck deep into the left arm
of Miura-no-Ishi Sakon-no-Taro, who was standing
about a tan behind Wada. "Ha-ha!" laughed Miura's
men as they came crowding round, "Wada-no-Kōtarō
boasts no one can equal him at shooting, and now he
has been put to shame openly." Then Yoshimori,
angered at this, sprang into a small boat and pressed
on into the midst of the foe, drawing his bow lustily
so that very many of his adversaries were killed and
wounded.

After this both sides set their faces against each
other and fought grimly without a thought for their
lives, neither giving way an inch. But as the Heike had
on their side an Emperor endowed with the Ten Virtues
and the Three Sacred Treasures of the Realm, things
went hard with the Genji and their hearts were beginning to fail them, when suddenly something that they
at first took for a white cloud, but which soon appeared to be a white banner floating in the breeze, came
drifting over the two fleets from the upper air and
finally settled on the stern of one of the Genji ships,
hanging on by the rope.

THE DROWNING OF THE EMPEROR

When he saw this, Yoshitsune, regarding it as a sign from Hachiman Dai-bosatsu, removed his helmet, and after washing his hands, did obeisance; his men all following his example. Moreover a shoal of some thousands of dolphins also made its appearance from the offing and made straight for the ships of the Heike. Then Munemori called the diviner Ko-hakase Harunobu and said: "There are always many dolphins about here, but I have never seen so many as these before; what may it portend?" "If they turn back," replied Harunobu, "the Genji will be destroyed; but if they go on then our own side will be in danger." No sooner had he finished speaking than the dolphins dived under the Heike ships and passed on.

Then, as things had come to this pass, Awa-no-Mimbu Shigeyoshi, who for three years had been a loyal supporter of the Heike, now that his son Dennai Saemon Noriyoshi had been captured, made up his mind that all was lost, and suddenly forsook his allegiance and deserted to the enemy. Great was the regret of Tomomori that he had not cut off the head of "that villain Shigeyoshi," but now it was unavailing.

Now the strategy of the Heike had been to put the stoutest warriors on board the ordinary fighting ships and the inferior soldiers on the big ships of Chinese build, so that the Genji should be induced to attack the big ships, thinking that the commanders were on board them, when they would be able to surround and destroy them. But when Shigeyoshi went over and joined the

Genji he revealed this plan to them, with the result that they immediately left the big ships alone and concentrated their attacks on the smaller ones on which were the Heike champions.

Later on the men of Shikoku and Kyūshū all left the Heike in a body and went over to the Genji. Those who had so far been their faithful retainers now turned their bows against their lords and drew the sword against their own masters. On one shore the heavy seas beat on the cliff so as to forbid any landing, while on the other stood the serried ranks of the enemy waiting with levelled arrows to receive them. And so on this day the struggle for supremacy between the houses of Gen and Hei was at last decided.

Meanwhile the Genji warriors sprang from one Heike vessel to the other, shooting and cutting down the sailors and helmsmen, so that they flung themselves in panic to the bottom of the ships unable to navigate them any longer. Then Shin-Chūnagon Tomomori rowed in a small boat to the Imperial Vessel and cried out: "You see what affairs have come to! Clean up the ship, and throw everything unsightly into the sea!" And he ran about the ship from bow to stern, sweeping and cleaning and gathering up the dust with his own hands. "But how goes the battle, Chūnagon Dono?" asked the Court Ladies. "Oh, you'll soon see some rare gallants from the East," he replied, bursting into loud laughter. "What? Is this a time for joking?" they answered, and they lifted up their voices and wept aloud.

Then the Nii Dono, who had already resolved what

she would do, donning a double outer dress of dark-grey mourning colour, and tucking up the long skirts of her glossy silk hakama, put the Sacred Jewel under her arm, and the Sacred Sword in her girdle, and taking the Emperor in her arms, spoke thus: "Though I am but a woman I will not fall into the hands of the foe, but will accompany our Sovereign Lord. Let those of you who will, follow me." And she glided softly to the gunwale of the vessel.

The Emperor was eight years old that year, but looked much older than his age, and his appearance was so lovely that he shed as it were a brilliant radiance about him, and his long black hair hung loose far down his back. With a look of surprise and anxiety on his face he inquired of the Nii Dono: "Where is it that you are going to take me?"

Turning to her youthful Sovereign with tears streaming down her cheeks, she answered: "Perchance our Lord does not know that, though through the merit of the Ten Virtues practised in former lives you have been reborn to the Imperial Throne in this world, yet by the power of some evil karma destiny now claims you. So now turn to the east and bid farewell to the deity of the Great Shrine of Ise, and then to the west and say the Nembutsu that Amida Buddha and the Holy Ones may come to welcome you to the Pure Western Land. This land is called small as a grain of millet, but yet is it now but a vale of misery. There is a Pure Land of happiness beneath the waves, another Capital where no sorrow is. Thither it is that I am taking our Lord."

Kiyomori's widow leaps into the sea with the
child-Emperor Antoku.

And thus comforting him, she bound his long hair up in his dove-coloured robe, and blinded with tears the child-Sovereign put his beautiful little hands together and turned first to the east to say farewell to the deity of Ise and to Sho-Hachimangū, and then to the west and repeated the Nembutsu, after which the Nii Dono, holding him tightly in her arms and saying consolingly: "In the depths of the Ocean we have a Capital" sank with him at last beneath the waves.

Ah, the pity of it! That the gust of the spring wind of Impermanence should so suddenly sweep away his flower form. That the cruel billows should thus engulf his Jewel Person. Since his Palace was called the Palace of Longevity, he should have passed a long life therein. Its gate was called the Gate of Eternal Youth, the barrier that old age should not pass; and yet, ere he had reached the age of ten years, he had become like the refuse that sinks to the bottom of the sea.

How vain it was to proclaim him as one who sat on the Throne as a reward of the Ten Virtues! It was like the Dragon that rides on the clouds descending to become a fish at the bottom of the ocean. He who abode in a Palace fair as the terraced pavilions of the highest heaven of Brahma, or the paradise where S'akya Muni dwells, among his Ministers and Nobles of the Nine Families who did him humble obeisance, thus came to a miserable end beneath the ocean waves.

The Death of Noto-no-kami

Now when the Imperial Consort Kenrei-mon-in saw what had come to pass, she put her inkstone and warming-stone into each side of the bosom of her robe and jumped into the sea. But Watanabe-no-Gengo Umanojo Mutsuru rowed up in a small boat, and clutching her long hair with a rake, dragged her back. Dainagon-no-suke-no-Tsubone, the wife of Shigehira, seeing this, cried out: "Alas! How cruel! How can you treat one who was an Empress in such a way?" So they informed Yoshitsune and he came in haste to the Imperial Vessel.

This Dainagon-no-suke had been just about to leap into the waves with the casket containing the Sacred Mirror, when an arrow pinned the skirt of her hakama to the side of the ship and she stumbled and fell, whereupon the Genji soldiers seized her and held her back. Then one of them wrenched off the lock of the casket to open it, when suddenly his eyes were darkened and blood poured from his nose. At this, Taira Dainagon Tokitada, who had been captured alive, and was standing by, exclaimed: "Hold! That is the Holy Naiji-dokoro, the Sacred Mirror that no profane eye must behold!" Whereat the soldiers were awe-stricken and trembled with fear; and the Hōgwan bade Tokitada-no-Kyō put away the casket as it was before.

Meanwhile Kadowaki Taira-no-Chūnagon Norimori and Shuri-no-Taiyū Tsunemori placed heavy anchors on their armour and hand in hand leapt into the sea. Komatsu-no-Shin-sammi Chūjō Sukemori, his brother

Komatsu-no-Shosho Arimori, and their cousin Sama-
no-kami Yukimori, also followed their example and
did likewise. But though the other members of the
family thus leapt into the waves, Munemori and his
son did not, but stood on the gunwale of the ship
looking round to see what would happen. Seeing them
thus hesitate, some of the Heike samurai, under pre-
tence of pushing by hurriedly, thrust Munemori over
into the sea, and his son, Uemon-no-kami Kiyomune,
seeing this, sprang in after him.

Now the others had put heavy objects on their
shoulders and held on to each other so that they might
be sure to sink, but these two did not do any such
thing, but, being good swimmers, they swam about
hither and thither, Munemori willing to sink or be
rescued whichever his son might do, when Ise Saburō
Yoshimori chanced to come up in a small boat and
drag Kiyomune out with a rake, after which Munemori
allowed himself to be pulled out also.

Now, as we have said, none could face the arrows
of Noto-no-kami Noritsune and live; and he had resolved to fight to the last this day. He was brilliantly
attired in a hitatare brocaded on a red ground, and a
suit of armour laced with Chinese silk; he wore a
helmet decorated with lofty horns, and a sword
mounted in gold and silver. In his quiver were twenty-
four arrows feathered with black and white feathers,
and with his Shigeto bow in his hand he shot them
hither and thither, killing and wounding many of the
foe. Then, when all his shafts were spent, he seized a
great black-lacquered two-handed sword in one hand

and a white-handled halberd in the other, and cut and slashed on all sides with reckless valour.

Then Shin-Chūnagon Tomomori despatched a messenger to him saying: "Why add to your sins by slaying so many men of little repute? Can you find no famous adversary?" "True," replied Noto-no-kami, "I will try a fall with some great Captain." And shortening his halberd in his hand he cut his way through the ships, dealing blows vigorously on every side, but as he did not recognize Yoshitsune he took another splendidly armed warrior for him and sprang across to engage him. Now Yoshitsune was fighting close by, but somehow or other did not turn to attack Noritsune. The latter, however, having thus chanced to spring on board his ship, suddenly espied him and made at him to grapple.

Yoshitsune, feeling himself unable to meet his on-set, stuck his halberd under his left arm and leaped nimbly over to one of the ships of his own side, a distance of full twenty feet. Noto-no-kami, less skilled in such tricks, was unable to follow him, and seeing that there was no more to be done, he tore off and flung away the sleeves and skirts of his armour, keeping only the breastplate, and, standing on the deck-house of the ship with his hair loose and dishevelled, he flung out his arms and shouted loudly: "Let any of the Genji who thinks himself somebody come forth and grapple with me and take me prisoner! I should like to go down to Kamakura and have a word with Yoritomo! Who'll come and try?" But there was none who answered his challenge.

Now there was a warrior named Aki-no-Taro Sane-mitsu, and he was so strong that he was said to possess the strength of twenty or thirty men. He had a retainer who was no less powerful than he, while his brother Jiro was also no ordinary warrior. "What is Noto Dono that we should fear him," they said; "he is no doubt a mighty warrior, but what of that? If he were a devil a hundred feet high, we three could settle him." And they got into a small boat and drew along-side the ship where Noritsune was, and boarded it and sprang at him together with their swords drawn.

Noritsune on his part sprang forward also, and seizing Aki-no-Taro's retainer who was foremost, kicked him into the sea; then, taking Aki-no-Taro himself under his left arm, and his brother Jiro under his right and gripping them tight, he sprang over into the waves, shouting: "Come along, both of you, to the Mountain of Death!" And he was twenty-six years old that year.

ENTRY OF THE SACRED MIRROR INTO THE CAPITAL

Then Shin-Chūnagon Tomomori, who had been watching how the day was going, at length saw that nothing remained but to put an end to his life, and call-ing his foster-brother Iga-no-Hei-naisaemon Ienaga, he said: "Is it not time to fulfil the promise we made?" "Certainly;" replied Ienaga. And he assisted Tomo-mori to don two suits of armour, afterwards doing the same himself, and the two leaped into the sea clasped in each other's arms. Some twenty samurai who were with them at once followed them into the waves; but

The end of Noto-no-kami Noritsune.

Etchū-no-Jirōhyōye Moritsugu, Kazusa-no-Gorōhyōye, Aku-shichibyōye Kagekiyo and Hida-no-Jirōhyōye, managed to elude the enemy somehow and escape.

And now the whole sea was red with the banners and insignia that they tore off and cut away, so that it looked like the waters of the Tatsuta-gawa when it is flecked with the maple leaves that the wind brings down in autumn, while the white breakers that rolled up on the beach were dyed a scarlet colour. The deserted empty ships rocked mournfully on the waves, driven aimlessly hither and thither by the wind and tide.

The former Udaijin Munemori Ko, Taira Dainagon Tokitada, Uemon-no-kami Kiyomune, Kura-no-kami Nobumoto, Sanuki-no-Chūgō, Tokizane and Mune-mori's eight year old son Hyobu-no-Sho Masaakira, were captured alive, beside the priests Nii-no-Sozu Senshin, Hosshoji-no-Shugyo No-en, Chūnagon-no-Risshi Chugai and Kyoju-bo-no-Ajari Yuen, and the samurai Gendaiyu-no-Hangwan Toshisada, Settsu-no-Hangwan Morizumi, Tonaisaemon-no-Jo Nobuyasu, Kitsunai-saemon-no-Jo Toshiyasu, and Awa-no-Mimbu Shigeyoshi and his son; thirty-eight in all. Kikuchi-no-Jirō Takanao and Harada-no-Taiyū Tanenao had already laid down their arms and surrendered before the battle. Forty-three Court Ladies were taken also, including the Imperial Consort Kenrei-mon-in, the foster-mother of the Emperor Takakura and wife of Rokujo Motozane, Ro-no-Onkata another daughter of Kiyomori, Dainagon-no-suke, Sotsu-no-suke, Jibu-Kyo-no-Tsubone and others; forty-three in all.

Thus by the fall of spring in the second year of Gen-ryaku,—a date of ill-omen indeed—the Emperor rested beneath the waves, while his Ministers and Courtiers tossed on the billows; the Imperial Consort and her Ladies were delivered into the hands of the Eastern barbarians to return to the Ancient Capital with all the Courtiers and Nobles as captives in the midst of myriads of foes, and their anguish must have been as deep as the regret of Chu Mai Ch'en at not wearing brocade, or the resentment of Wang Chao Chun when she set out for the land of the Tartars.

On the third day of the fourth month Kurō Hōgwan Yoshitsune dispatched Genpachi Hirotsuna as a messenger to the Hō-ō with the tidings that: "On the twenty-fourth day of the third month at the Hour of the Hare, at Ta-no-ura and Moji-ga-seki in the province of Buzen, and at Dan-no-ura and Akamagaseki in the province of Nagato, the Heike have been completely annihilated, and the Sacred Mirror and Sacred Seal will forthwith be returned to the Capital." When the Hō-ō heard this news he was exceedingly pleased, and calling Hirotsuna into the courtyard, demanded to be told all details of the battle, in his joy conferring on him the title of Sahyōye on the spot. On the fifth day His Majesty ordered To-Hōgwan Nobumori, one of the Imperial Guard, to go and see that the two Sacred Emblems were properly brought back; so he took one of the Imperial Horses and set off at full speed for the Western Provinces without even delaying to go back to his lodging.

Concerning Rokudai

Now Hōjō-no-Shiro Tokimasa was made Warden of Miyako to represent Yoritomo there, and in order that none of the male posterity of the Heike should escape him, he made proclamation that anyone, high or low, who could give him any information as to their whereabouts, should receive whatever he might wish. And regrettable to say, many in the Capital, anxious to gain rewards, made search and gave information, so that many were discovered.

So much so that they seized upon even the children of the lowest servants, if they were handsome and of fair complexion, declaring: "This is the son of such and such a Chūjō, or: "This is the heir of such and such a Shosho:" and when the mother or father wept and lamented, they would say: "The foster-mother has said so;" or: "His nurse has told us:" and if they were quite young children they would be thrown into the water or buried alive, or if they were older they would be strangled or stabbed, so that the grief and lamentation of their mothers and foster-mothers was beyond compare. Hōjō himself was pained at this wholesale slaughter, but as he had to obey orders he could do nothing.

Among these descendants was Rokudai Gozen, the heir of Komatsu-Chūjō Koremori, who was now growing up, and as he was the grandson and heir, he searched everywhere to try and find him and put him to death, but all to no effect, and he was just about to return to Kamakura with his purpose unfulfilled, when a certain woman came to Rokuhara and said: "Westward from here, at a place called Shōbudani, to the north of the mountain temple of Daigakuji which lies behind Henjoji, the wife and children of Komatsu-Chūjō Koremori are in hiding."

Hōjō was exceedingly pleased to hear this, and immediately sent some one to spy out the place. Going thither he found that in a certain temple building, there were several women and children carefully concealed, and as he peeped through a chink in the fence he saw a white puppy run out, followed by a very handsome boy; then a woman who looked like his foster-mother came out hurriedly and drew him in again, exclaiming: "How terrible if anyone should see you!" This is certainly he, thought the spy, as he hastened back and told what he had seen, and the next day Hōjō surrounded Shōbudani with soldiers and sent a messenger to the temple saying: "I have heard that Rokudai Gozen, the son of Komatsu-no-sammi Chūjō Koremori, is in this place, and Hōjō-no-Shiro Tokimasa, the representative of Kamakura Dono, wishes to see him, so please bring forth at once."

When his mother heard this her senses reeled so that for a while she knew nothing, and Saito Go and Saito Roku, the child's two faithful retainers, tried to find some way to escape with him, but when they saw the soldiers surrounding them on all sides, they knew it was no use.

So as it must be, his mother dressed him and smoothed his hair, weeping as she did so, and just before he started she put into his hand a beautiful little rosary

Rokudai is discovered.

of black wood, saying: "Take this, and be sure you repeat the Nembutsu as often as you can, that you may go to Paradise." "Since I must part with you to-day," replied the boy as he took it, "I wish if possible to go where my father is." At this his younger sister, who was about ten years old, cried out also: "I too want to go and see my father;" and she ran out after him, so that the foster-mother had to hold her back.

Rokudai Gozen was twelve years old, but looked more grown up than most boys of fourteen or fifteen, and was very handsome and charming in his disposition. He tried hard to show a bold front to the enemy, but his tears ran down under the sleeve that he pressed to his face as he got into the palanquin, which then moved off surrounded by soldiers on all sides. Saito Go and Saito Roku walked on each side of their young master, and though Hōjō made two of his men get off their horses for them to ride, they declined, and walked barefoot all the way from Daigakuji to Rokuhara. His mother and the other lady flung themselves on the ground, gazing up to heaven in an agony of longing.

Then the foster-mother, impelled by restlessness of spirit, wandered out of the Daigakuji and was walking about aimlessly in the vicinity, weeping as she went, when she met some one who told her that behind there dwelt a priest of the mountain temple of Takao, called Mongaku, who was very much trusted by Yoritomo in all matters, and that he wished to find a son of some Court lady to become his disciple. At this she was overjoyed, and at once making her way to Takao she begged to see Mongaku and thus addressed him, weeping bitterly the while: "My young lord, whom I have carried in my arms since he was born, and who is now twelve years old, was yesterday carried away by the soldiers. Could not your reverence beg his life, and bring him up as your disciple?" And she fell down before the monk, weeping unrestrainedly, so that he knew not what to do.

Feeling compassion for her distress he asked her who the boy was. "It is the beloved child of the wife of Komatsu-Chūjō Koremori," she replied, "and we were bringing him up, but somebody must have said that he was the son of the Chūjō, so yesterday the soldiers came and took him." "Who was the warrior who took him?" asked the priest.. "He said his name was Hōjō-no-Shiro Tokimasa;" replied the lady. "Well I will go and see him;" declared Mongaku, and he went off there and then.

So the priest went to Rokuhara and asked about the matter. "It is the order of Kamakura Dono," said Hōjō, "that every one of the male descendants of the Heike should be sought out and put to death, and among them is Rokudai Gozen, son of Komatsu-Chūjō Koremori. Unexpectedly I received news of him the day before yesterday, and yesterday went and brought him here; but indeed he is such a beautiful child that I am sorry I did not leave him where he was."

"Well, may I see him?" asked Mongaku, and when he was taken to where the child was, he found him dressed in a double embroidered hitatare, holding in his hand the rosary of black wood. Such was the beauty of his hair and the elegance and nobility of his form and bearing, that he hardly looked like a creature of this world at all. Though his face was a little thin, and he had perchance not slept much that night, yet he looked indeed very lovable.

When the child caught sight of the priest his eyes filled with tears for some reason or other, and Mongaku too moistened the sleeve of his black robe. "However great an enemy he might become in the future," he thought "how could anyone put him to death now?" Then, turning to Hōjō, he said: "It is no doubt a matter connected with a previous existence, but when I consider this child I am filled with a great pity for him. Will you not grant him a reprieve for twenty days, while I go down to Kamakura and obtain a pardon for him?

"When I went up to the Capital in former days to procure an Imperial Edict to establish the position of Yoritomo, as I travelled all night through the plains around the Fujikawa, I lost my way and was nearly washed away and drowned, and then after that I met with robbers in Mount Takashi, and barely escaping with my life managed to effect an entrance into the 'Prison Palace' of Fukuhara and receive the Edict from the Hō-ō. In recognition of this service Yoritomo promised that whatever request I might make of him at any time, he would surely grant it, and moreover I have done him many important services since then. It is no new thing that I say, but as I have valued my duty more than my life, Yoritomo will not

forget it, unless his high position has puffed him up."
And he set out for Kamakura at the dawn of that day.

Saito Go and Saito Roku, regarding the monk as a
living Buddha indeed, pressed their hands together and
wept. They then returned to Daigakuji and acquainted
the child's mother with all that had happened, to her
very great joy. With regard to the decision of Yoritomo, they were in suspense as to what it would be,
but were cheered by his life being spared for twenty
days, and ascribing it to the power of Kwannon of
Hase, they put their trust in that deity. So things went
on, and the twenty days sped by like a dream, but the
monk did not come back. "How can this be?" they
said with sinking hearts, and all their grief and anxiety
assailed them once again. Hōjō also, as the twenty
days that he had agreed to wait had passed, thought
that Yoritomo had probably refused the pardon, and
fretted impatiently at the delay, for he wished to start
immediately for Kamakura.

So at dawn on the seventeenth day of the twelfth
month Hōjō-no-Shiro Tokimasa took the child
Rokudai Gozen and departed from Miyako. Saito Go
and Saito Roku went with him, walking on each side
of the palanquin. Again Hōjō bade two of his men
dismount that they might ride, but they declined saying: "As it is the last time we are quite content;" and
so they went their way barefoot, weeping tears of
blood. Thus pitifully parted from his mother and
nurse, looking back on the Imperial City as it lay beyond the clouds, as for the last time he set out on the

road to the far-off Eastern Provinces, the state of the child's feelings can well be imagined.

If one of the samurai quickened his pace, his heart sank, thinking he was coming to cut off his head; and if one of them chanced to speak to him: "Now is the end," he would guess in dismay. He thought it might be at Shi-no-miya-kawara, but they passed on through Sekiyama and came to the beach of Otsu. He wondered if it would not be at Awazu-no-hara, but by that time the dusk had already fallen. And so they went on, station by station and province by province until they came to the province of Suruga, where it seemed that his fleeting life would end.

At a place called Sembon-no-matsubara the palanquin was set down and the young lord ordered to get out, a leather mat being spread for him to sit on. Then Hōjō hastily sprang from his horse, and approaching the child spoke as follows: "I have brought you thus far because I thought we might meet the monk on the way, but if I take you over the Hakone mountains I know not what Kamakura Dono would say. So I shall say that I executed you in the province of Ōmi. As this was foreordained from a previous life, how is it possible anyhow to escape it?"

Then the young lord, seeing that his time was come, pulled back with his beautiful little hand the long hair that hung about his shoulders, whereat the soldiers of the guard exclaimed: "See how he is yet master of himself;" and they all moistened the sleeves of their armour. Then, looking toward the west, he joined his hands together, and repeating the Nembutsu in a loud

Mongaku saves Rokudai.

voice ten times, stretched out his neck for the blow. Then Kudo Saburo Chikatoshi, who had been chosen as the executioner, seized his sword and moved round behind him from the left, and was just about to strike, when his eyes darkened and his senses reeled, so that he could not see where to aim his weapon. "I cannot do it," he exclaimed, hardly knowing what he did: "pray choose some one else;" and he threw down his sword and withdrew.

Then as they cast about to find some one to take his place, there appeared a priest in black robes, riding a cream-coloured horse which he was whipping up furiously; and as the people round about called out to him: "See the handsome young lord whom Hōjō Dono is just beheading in the pine-wood," and ran thronging to see the sight, he waved his whip at them anxiously, and in his excitement and suspense pulled off his hat and beckoned to them with it.

Then, as Hōjō stood waiting to see what was the reason, the priest rode up, sprang down from his horse and exclaimed: "The young lord is reprieved; here are instructions from Yoritomo." Hōjō took the document and read: "Concerning Rokudai Gozen, the son of Komatsu-no-sammi Chūjō Koremori, whom you have arrested: he is reprieved at the request of Mongaku, the priest of Takao; let there be no mistake. To Hōjō-no-Shiro Dono. Yoritomo." Hōjō read it through several times, ejaculating: "Marvellous! Marvellous!" and then put it away. Saito Go and Saito Roku, it is unnecessary to say, and even Hōjō's own retainers, shed tears of joy and relief.

THE EXECUTION OF ROKUDAI

So Rokudai Gozen grew up thus until he was fourteen or fifteen years old, when he was so beautiful that he shed as it were a radiance all about him. But that his mother should have said in admiration: "If we were in power he would now be an officer of the Imperial Guard," was too outspoken. At a favourable opportunity Yoritomo sent to Mongaku saying: "What kind of youth is Rokudai Gozen, son of the Sammi Chūjō Koremori whom you have in charge? Do you think of him as you did of me formerly, that he is one able to subdue the enemies of the Throne, or avenge his father's shame?" "Do not trouble yourself about him," replied Mongaku, "for he is a spiritless and stupid fellow."

Still Kamakura Dono was not quite satisfied. "If there were a rebellion that priest would be for it," he remarked ominously; "and though it is not likely in my lifetime, I don't know about my posterity." When this reached his mother's ear she again urged him to become a monk without further delay. So, about the spring of the fifth year of Bun-ji, cutting off his beautiful hair short at the neck, and attired in a robe and hakama of drab colour, with his travelling box on his back, he started out on a pilgrimage; and Saito Go and Saito Roku accompanied their master in similar garb.

First ascending Mount Kōya, he visited Takiguchi Nyūdō, the virtuous priest who had helped his father to attain Enlightenment and instructed him in the Way, and from him heard all particulars of his father's becoming a monk, and his subsequent death. Then, wishing to retrace his father's steps, he went on to Kumano, and looking across at the island of Yamanari which is in front of the shrine called Hama-no-miya, to which his father had rowed, he greatly desired to cross over to it, but on account of the contrary wind he was not able. As he stood gazing over at it he wondered in what place it was that his father had sunk, and felt as though he wished to ask the white-crested waves that came rolling in on the shore. Regarding the sand of the beach tenderly, as being perchance the bones of his parent, his sleeves were bedraggled with tears, and ever moist like those of the sea-damp garments of the fishermen. Passing all that night on the beach, he spent his time reading the Sutras and repeating the Nembutsu, drawing with his finger the likeness of a Buddha in the sand; and when dawn appeared, summoning a priest, he dedicated all the merit he had acquired to the enlightenment of his father's spirit, and returned to the Capital with his heart full of sadness.

Now the Emperor at this time was Go-Toba-no-in, and he thought of nothing but pleasure, so that all the affairs of state were in the hands of the mother of the Empress, and people lamented greatly at it. Because the King of Wu loved Chien K'e, those who suffered hurt in the kingdom were not few; and because Hsi Yao captivated the King of Tsu many ladies of the Court died of starvation. And because those of lower rank will always imitate the pleasures of those above them, all those of understanding loudly lamented the danger to the Empire. But the second Imperial Prince

Go-Takakura-in was much devoted to statesmanship, and very diligent in intellectual matters, and Mongaku, shrewd priest that he was, was very fond of meddling in the management of affairs, so that he was extremely anxious to set this Prince on the Throne; but while Yoritomo was alive, he did not take any steps.

Then, on the thirteenth day of the first month of the tenth year of Kenkyu, Yoritomo died at the age of fifty-three, and Mongaku raised a revolt forthwith; but it was immediately discovered, and officers were sent to Nijo Inokuma to arrest Mongaku, who was then more than eighty years of age, and banish him to the province of Oki. As they were leading him away from the Capital he burst out: "What does that Ball-loving Youth mean by letting them take an old man like me, who does not know whether he will live from one day to the next, and send him under Imperial Chastisement to a place like Oki, far away from the Capital. You had better see that some one is sent there to bring me back pretty quickly!"

And so, dancing with rage and reviling strongly, Mongaku was sent into exile. It was because this Emperor was so fond of playing ball that Mongaku called him by this contemptuous name. It was very strange that afterwards, in the period Shō-kyū, on account of his many rebellions, though there were many other provinces, this Emperor should have also been banished to the far-off isles of Oki. And it is said that the angry ghost of Mongaku wrought many evil things there; continually appearing in the Emperor's Presence, and saying all kinds of things to him.

Now Rokudai Gozen, who was now styled Sammi-no-Zenji, had continued to live in retirement in the recesses of Takao. "The son of such a man, and the disciple of such a man," quoth Yoritomo, "though he may have shaved his head, is not likely to have shaved his heart." And he sent a petition to the Court that he might be taken and executed, and An-Hōgwan Sukekane arrested him and sent him down to the Eastern Provinces, where Okabe Yasutsuna of the province of Suruga was ordered to take him and behead him at Tagoe-gawa in the province of Sagami. That his life was spared from his thirteenth year to beyond his thirtieth was solely through the mercy of Kwannon of Hase. And with the death of Sammi-no-Zenji there perished the last of the Heike.

The Former Empress becomes a Nun

The Former Empress Kenrei-mon-in went to Yoshida at the foot of Higashi-yama, and entered the cell of a monk of Nara called Chūnagon-no-Hōin Keiei. It was old and dilapidated, with the garden overgrown with weeds, and hare's-foot fern clustering thickly on the roof. The curtains were gone and the bedchamber exposed, and there was nothing to keep out the wind and rain. Though there were many kinds of flowers, there was none to care for them, and though the moon streamed in every night, no one was there to gaze at it.

She, who had formerly spent her time in the Jewel Halls and within the Brocade Curtain, now suffered the unspeakable hardships of dwelling in this mouldering cell, bereft of all her old companions, like a fish on the dry land or a bird torn from its nest, and she yearned fondly for the times she had spent tossing on the heaving billows. In the words of the poet Tachibana Chokkan: "She longs for the far-off waves of the ocean, and the clouds of the limitless Western Sea; the moss grows thick on the reed-thatched hut; tears fall as the moon shines in the garden on Higashi-yama."

So on the first day of the fifth month of the first year of Bun-ji, the Former Empress cut short her hair and was instructed in the Way by Ashōbō-no-Shonin Insei of Chōrakuji, and for the customary offering she presented him with the robe of the Emperor Antoku, which he had worn up to the time of his death, so that the perfume yet clung to it. She had brought it with her to the Capital from the far-off Western Provinces, intending to keep it as a memorial of him and never let it leave her person, but now, as she had nothing else to offer, and thinking moreover that it would be an aid to his Enlightenment, weeping bitterly she handed it to him. The monk was so affected that he could utter no word, but pressing the sleeve of his black robe to his face, he retired weeping from the Imperial Presence. And this robe was afterwards woven into a banner and suspended in front of the Buddha of the Chōrakuji.

This Empress was appointed Imperial Consort at the age of fifteen, and at sixteen was raised to the rank of Empress. She was ever by the Emperor's side, helping him in the government by day, and the only sharer of his love by night. At the age of twenty-two she bore a Prince who was named as the Heir to the Throne, and when he assumed the Imperial Dignity she became Retired Empress and took the name of Kenrei-mon-in. She was the daughter of the Lay-priest Chancellor Kiyomori, and as she had thus become the mother of the Emperor she was held in great reverence by all the people.

She was twenty-nine years old this year, and the beauty of her fair face was not yet dimmed, neither was the elegance of her slender form impaired; but what now availed the loveliness of her hair? So she renounced this world and became a nun, but even when she had entered the True Way her grief was not assuaged. Ever she seemed to see before her the figures of the Emperor and the Nii Dono and the others as they sank in the waves, and never in this life could she forget those melancholy scenes, so she wondered why she had remained alive to bear such sorrows, and her tears were never dried.

Even in the short nights of the fifth month, it was not easy to keep awake, but if she did not fall asleep she did not dream of those who had passed away. Faintly the shadow of her single light fell on the wall outside, and all night the dismal drumming of the rain sounded on the lattice of the windows. Surely the Imperial Consorts who were shut up in the Shang Yang Palace in China were not more wretched. And how did it remind her of the beloved past, this orange-tree in blossom by the eaves, that the former tenant had brought and planted there. As its heavy perfume was wafted into her chamber, and the note of the cuckoo was borne once and again to her ears, this ancient verse came into her mind, and she wrote it on the lid of her inkstone:

> Hark! The cuckoo's call,
> Seeking out the fragrant scent
> Of the orange flowers.
> "Where are those I loved of old?
> Whither have they flown?" he cries.

The rest of the Court Ladies, who had thrown themselves into the sea, but had not drowned themselves with the same determination as the Nii Dono and the wife of Echizen-no-sammi Michimori, had been roughly dragged out by the Genji soldiers and brought back to the Capital, as has been before related. And these, both young and old, all became nuns and were living in concealment in far-away valleys and dells in the mountains, wretched and emaciated in appearance and quite unrecognizable as their former selves. The places where they lived have gone up in smoke, and the empty site is all that remains. They have all turned into overgrown moorland, and no former intimate ever comes nigh them. All is as unfamiliar as his home to one who is bewitched by fairies and returns to it after seven generations.

The Former Empress goes to Ohara

Now as her poor abode was ruined in the great earthquake of the ninth day of the seventh month, and its outer wall fell down, the Former Empress had nowhere to live. How had the days altered from when the green-clad Palace Guards stood continually before her gate, for now the tumble-down wall, more bedewed with moisture than the outside moorland, seemed as if it understood the change of times, and resented the incessant shrilling of the insects. So though the nights grew longer and longer, the Empress could not sleep, but brooded continually over her melancholy condition, and this, added to the natural sadness of autumn, became almost too much for her to bear. In this changed world there was none to feel sympathy for her, and all those of her affinity were gone, so that none were left to cherish her in her need.

Only the wife of Reizei-no-Dainagon Takafusa and the wife of Shichijo-no-Shuri-no-Taiyū Nobutaka used to send and assist her secretly. "Ah," she exclaimed, "in former days who would have ever dreamed that I should have come to accept anything from such as these?" And as she wept afresh at the thought, the ladies who accompanied her could not refrain from moistening their sleeves. Since her present dwelling was too near the Capital, and attracted the eyes of curious passers-by, she thought she would like to go to some place far away in the depths of the mountains to spend her days remote from all sound of unrest, but for some time she was unable to hear of any.

Then a certain lady came to Yoshida and said to her: "There is a place northward from here, in the mountains of Ohara, called Jakkō-in, and it is very quiet." "A mountain abode is very lonely, it is true," she answered, "but it is good to live in, for it is remote from the troubles of this world." So, as she desired it, the matter was settled, and the wives of Nobutaka and Takafusa sent a palanquin to fetch her.

Thus at the end of the ninth month she proceeded to the temple of Jakkō-in. As they went along she gazed at the beauty of the autumn tints, while the sun sank gradually behind the mountains. The dreary boom of the evening bell of the wayside temple, and the thick-lying dew on the grass as they passed drew tears from her eyes, while the fierce gale whirled the leaves from the trees in all directions. Suddenly the sky grew dark and the autumn drizzle began to fall; the cry of a deer sounded faintly and the shrilling of the insects was incessant. Nothing was wanting to add to the sum of her afflictions, which seemed indeed such as few had been made to suffer. Even when she was driven about from shore to shore and from island to island her melancholy was not to be compared to this.

The place she had chosen to dwell in was ancient and surrounded by mossy rocks; the reeds in the garden were now covered with hoar-frost instead of dew. and when she gazed on the faded hue of the withered chrysanthemums by the wall, she could hardly fail to be reminded of her own condition. Entering before the Buddha she prayed: "For the Sacred Spirit of the Emperor, that it may attain perfect Buddhahood, and for the departed spirits of all the Heike, that they may quickly enter the Way of Salvation." But still the image of the late Emperor was impressed on her mind, and wherever she might be, she thought she could never forget it.

So they built for her a small cell ten feet square beside the Jakkō-in, and in it were two rooms, in one of which she put her shrine of Buddha, and in the other she slept; and there she spent her time continually repeating the Nembutsu and performing the Buddhist services, both by night and by day. And it happened that once, on the fifth day of the tenth month, she heard the sound as of some one treading on the oak leaves which had fallen and covered the garden. "Who can it be," she exclaimed, "that comes to disturb one who has thus renounced the world? Do you go and see; for I will conceal myself if it be anyone I do not wish to meet." So one of the ladies went to look, and it was only a young stag that had passed that way. "Who is it? Who is it?" asked the Empress, whereupon the lady Dainagon-no-suke-no-Tsubone composed these lines in reply:

> Since you thus inquire
> Who it is that strays this way,
> Rustling in the leaves.
> 'Tis no human visitor,
> But a stag that haunts the vale.

And the Empress was so much affected by this verse that she wrote it on the paper of the sliding door.

And as she thus passed her tedious hours, even in this dreary spot she found many subjects for comparison. The trees that grew by the eaves of her cell she likened to the Seven Precious Trees of Paradise, and the water that collected in the hollows of the rocks she compared to the Lake of the Eight Virtues in the Pure Land. Impermanence is as the flowers of spring that so quickly fall when the wind blows, and Worldly Illusion like the moon of autumn so easily lost behind the clouds. She thought how she had diverted herself with the flowers in the Shōyōden, and how on the day after they had been scattered by the wind, and how in the Chōshuden they had made poems to the moon, and its light had been hidden by the clouds. Formerly she had lived delicately in the Jewel Halls, and couches of brocade had been spread for her in the Golden Palace, but now she dwelt in a hut of brushwood and thatch, and the sleeves of her robe were dishevelled and tear-stained.

The Hō-ō Proceeds to Ohara

Thus in the spring of the second year of Bun-ji the Hō-ō expressed a wish to go to Ohara and see the place where Kenrei-mon-in was living in retirement, but the second and third months were stormy and the cold still lingered, neither did the snow melt on the mountains nor the icicles thaw in the valleys. Thus the spring passed and the summer came, and the festival of Kamo was already over when His Majesty proceeded to the recesses of Ohara. Though the visit was incognito, the Sadaisho Tokudaiji, the Dainagon Kwazan-in and the Gon-Chūnagon Tsuchi-mikado accompanied His Majesty, with six of the higher Courtiers and eight of lower rank, beside several of the Imperial Guards.

As they went by way of Kurama, His Majesty was able to visit the temple of Fudarakuji, built at Fuka-yabu at Kiyohara, and the place where the Consort of the Emperor Go-Reizei-in had formerly lived in retirement at Ono, after which the Imperial Palanquin proceeded on its way. The white clouds on the distant mountains reminded them of the cherry-blossoms that had fallen, while the green leaves on the twigs seemed to regret the passing of spring. It was past the twentieth day of the fourth month, so the summer grasses had grown up thickly, and as they parted them on the little-trodden road, His Majesty, who had never been there before, was much affected by the lonely uninhabited look of the place.

At the foot of the western mountains they came to a small temple. This was the Jakkō-in. It might be well described by the lines: "Its roof-tiles were broken and mist was its only incense; the doors had fallen from their hinges and the beams of the moon were its sanctuary lamps." But the pond and trees of its ancient garden were dignified; the young grass had grown thick, and the slender shoots of the willow were all hanging in confusion, while the floating waterplants on the pond might be mistaken for spread out brocade. On the island the purple hue of the flowering wistaria mingled with the green of the pine-tree, while the late-blooming cherry among the green leaves was more rare than the early blossoms. From the eightfold clouds of the kerria that was flowering in profusion on the bank came the call of the cuckoo, a note of welcome in honour of His Majesty's visit.

When the Hō-ō saw it he composed these lines:

> Lo! the cherry-tree
> Leaning o'er the silent depths
> Of the garden pool
> While the fallen petals float
> On the gently rippling wave!

Pleasant was the sound of the water as it fell from the

clefts of the time-worn rocks, and the ivied walls and beetling crags would have defied the brush of the painter. When His Majesty came to the cell of the former Empress, ivy was growing on the eaves and the morning-glory was climbing up them; the hare's-foot fern and the day-lily mingled together, and here and there was a useless gourd-plant. Here was the grass that grew thick in the path of Yen Yuan, and the white goose-foot that keeps men at a distance, and here too was the rain that moistened the door of Yuan Hsien.

The cedar boards of the roof were gaping, so that the rain, the hoar-frost, and the dew of evening vied with the moonbeams in gaining entrance, and the place appeared wellnigh uninhabitable. Behind was the mountain and in front was the moor, and the bamboo grasses rustled loudly in the wind. As is the way with those who have no friends in the world, she seldom heard any news from the Capital, but what she did hear was the cry of the monkeys as they sprang from tree to tree, and the sound of the wood-cutter's axe, for few people there were that came there.

Then the Hō-ō called to the inmate, but there was no answer, but after a while a withered-looking old nun appeared of whom he inquired: "Whither has the former Empress deigned to go?" "Over there to the mountain to pick some flowers," was the reply. "How hard it is," said His Majesty, "that since she has thus renounced the world, she has no one to perform such services for her." "Since this fate has come upon her in accordance with the Five Precepts and the Ten Vir-

The Hō-ō Go-Shirakawa at the temple of Jakkō-in.

tues," replied the nun, "why should she spare herself the austerities of mortifying her flesh?

"In the Ingwa Kyō it is written: 'If you wish to know the cause in the former life, look at the effect in the present life; and if you wish to know the effect in the future life, look at the cause in the present one.' And if she knows the cause and effect of both past and future lives, there is nothing at all for her to lament. In former days Prince Siddartha at the age of nineteen went forth from Gaya and dwelt at the foot of Mount Dantaloka; covering himself with the leaves of trees, going up the peaks to get firewood and down into the valleys to draw water, by the merit of his austerities and mortifications at last he attained to perfect Buddha-hood."

Looking at this nun the Hō-ō noticed that she was clothed in pieces of silk and cotton put together roughly anyhow, and thinking it strange that one of such an appearance should speak thus, he asked her who she was. For some time she could answer nothing, but only wept, but after a while she controlled her feelings and replied: "I am ashamed to say so, but I am Awa-no-Naiji, daughter of the late Shonagon Nyūdō Shinzei, and my mother was Kii-no-Nii. As your Majesty was formerly so kind to me, the reason why you do not now recognize me must be that I have become old and in-firm." And she pressed her sleeve to her face, unable to control herself any longer: a sad sight indeed.

"Can it be so?" exclaimed the Hō-ō; "and you are truly Awa-no-Naiji? I did not recognize you, but however one may think, it all seems like a dream."

And his voice became choked with sobs, while the Courtiers who accompanied him were moved also, some saying that what she said was very strange, while others thought it quite natural. And the Hō-ō looked about him hither and thither, and the plants of the garden, heavy with dew, fell against the boundary wall, and the surface of the rice-fields was covered with water so that there seemed not even room for a snipe to perch; and His Majesty went to the cell of the former Empress and opened the shōji and looked in.

In one chamber were the images of the three Bosatsu, Amida, Kwannon, and Seishi, and in the hand of Amida, who stood in the middle, was a cord of five colours. On the left was a picture of Fugen and on the right of Zendo Kwasho, beside which hung a portrait of the late Emperor. There were also eight rolls of the Hokke Kyō and nine volumes of the Amida Kyō. Instead of the perfume of orchids and musk, the smoke of incense filled the air. The merit of Vimalakirrti, who in a nine-foot-square cell ranged in order thirty-two thousand floors and invited all the Buddhas of the Ten Quarters, could hardly have been greater.

On the shōji were stuck texts from all the Sutras, written on coloured paper, and among them was one written at Ch'ing Li'ang Shan in China by Oe-no-Sadamoto, which ran thus: "Sounds of celestial melody are heard afar off, and from the regions of the setting sun Amida comes to save mankind." A little removed from these was a verse that seemed to be from the former Empress's own pen:

Could I e'er have dreamed
That from such a spot as this
I should view the moon—
Then, the stately Palace halls,
Now, this lonely mountain cell.

Then on the other side he saw what appeared to be
her bed-chamber. On a bamboo pole hung her robes
of hempen cloth, besides some bed-quilts of paper,
and when he thought of the countless beautiful robes
of silk gauze and rich brocade, wrought of the stuffs
both of China and of her own land, that she had worn in
the dream-like days of her dominion, the tears coursed
down his Imperial cheeks, and the Courtiers of his
escort also could not help moistening their sleeves at
these evidences of her altered condition.

Presently two nuns clad in dark robes were seen
making their way slowly and painfully down through
the rough rocks of the mountain-side, and on the Hō-ō
inquiring who they were, the old nun replied: "The
one carrying a basket of mountain-azaleas on her arm
is the former Empress, and the one who has the load
of bracken for firewood is Dainagon-no-suke-no-
Tsubone, the daughter of Torikai-no-Chūnagon Kore-
zane, and adopted daughter of Gōjō-no-Dainagon
Kunitsuna, who was nurse to the late Emperor." As
she spoke she burst into tears, and the Hō-ō and his
Courtiers also applied their sleeves to their eyes.

The former Empress, since she was living apart from
the world in this way, was so overwhelmed with shame
at seeing them that she would gladly have hidden herself somewhere to avoid them, but she could not. Every
evening she girt up her long sleeves to draw the water

for the offering, and early every morning they were wet and bedraggled with the mountain dew. So, as she could not again retrace her steps to the mountain, neither was she able to get into her cell, the old nun came to her as she stood dumbfounded and took her basket from her hands.

THE SIX PATHS*

"Since you have renounced the world," said Awa-no-Naiji, "what does it matter about your appearance? I pray you come and greet His Majesty, for he will soon return." So the former Empress repressed her emotion and entered her cell. "Before my window in prayer I await the coming of Amida," she said, "and at my lowly door I look for the Saviour of mankind; but Your Majesty's gracious visit I did not expect."

The Hō-ō, looking upon her, thus replied: "Even those who live for eighty thousand kalpas in the highest heaven of the World of Formlessness must surely die, and the denizens of the Six Celestial Worlds of Desire cannot escape the Five Changes. The wondrous bliss of the city of delight of the heavens of Indra, and the passionless serenity of the high pavilions of the mid-Dyana world of the heavens of Brahma, even these, like the rewards of dreamland or the pleasures of a vision, eternally change and dissolve, turning and revolving like the wheels of a chariot. And since the Celestial Beings are subject to the Five Changes, how shall men escape? But I hope that you still hear

_____

*Hell, Pretas, Beasts, Asuras, Men, and Heaven.

tidings from your old acquaintances, for you must
think much of old times."

"There are none from whom I hear anything now,"
replied the Empress, "except from the wives of Nobutaka and of Takafusa, who continually send me help;
but in former days I never even dreamed of being assisted by people such as they." And as she spoke her
tears flowed, and her lady companions also hid their
faces in their sleeves.

After a while she controlled her emotion and continued: "Though I need not say that being reduced
to such a condition has been a great grief to me, yet I
feel gladness on account of my enlightenment in the
next world. By the help of S'akya Muni, reverently
relying on the Great Vow of Amida, I may escape the
troubles of the Five Hindrances and the Three Obe-
diences, and in this latter age purify the Six Senses,
so that, fixing my hopes on the highest heaven, and
fervently praying for the enlightenment of our whole
family, I may await the coming of the Saving Host.

"But the thing that I can never forget is the image
of the late Emperor, and even though I try to bear his
loss with patience, I cannot, for truly there is nothing
that wrings the heart like parental affection. And so I
pass both day and night in ceaseless prayer for his enlightenment, and this will be my guide also in the True
Way." "Verily this our Empire is but a petty country,"
answered the Hō-ō, "but since by observance of the
Ten Virtues he became its Emperor, everything must
be in accordance with his will. And though all who
are born in an age when the Law of Buddha has been

widely spread, if they have the desire to practise the Law, without doubt will be hereafter reborn in bliss, yet when I regard your present condition, though it is in accordance with the vanity of human affairs, I cannot but be overcome with grief." And as he spoke His Majesty burst into tears.

"Born the daughter of the Taira Chancellor," continued the former Empress, "and having become the mother of the Emperor, the whole Empire lay in the hollow of my hand. Clad in my varied robes of state, from the New Year Festival to the Year End Ceremonies I was surrounded by the Great Ministers and Courtiers in brilliant throng, even as above the clouds the Six Heavens of Desire and the Four Dhyana Heavens are encircled by eight myriads of lesser heavens.

"Dwelling in the Seiryōden and the Shishinden behind the Jewel Curtain, I gladdened my eyes in spring with the blossoms of the Imperial Cherry Tree. In the hot months of summer I refreshed myself with crystal streams, and in the autumn I viewed the moon in the midst of my ladies. In the cold nights of winter soft bed-quilts were heaped up to warm me, and I thought that I had only to wish for the draught of immortality, and the magic potion of eternal life and youth brought from Horai the Elysian isle, for it to be immediately forthcoming. So full was my life of joy and happiness, both by day and by night, that perchance even in heaven nothing could surpass it.

"Then in the autumn of Ju-ei when Yoshinaka came up to attack us, after setting fire to their ancient homes, our family fled from the Capital where they had lived so long, looking sadly back at the Imperial Palace. Going down to the shore of Suma and Akashi, of which I before knew only the name, we set sail on the boundless ocean, and so from island to island and from shore to shore, our sleeves wet with the salt spray by day, and the cry of the sea-birds mingling with our sobs by night, we rowed about seeking some favourable refuge, but never forgetting our ancient home. Left thus with none to help us, the anguish of the Five Changes of our dissolution came upon us. We speak of the 'Pain of the Grief of Parting' and the 'Pain of the Regret of Meeting,' and both of these in one I have known to the full. For when we came to Dazaifu in the island of Kyushu, thinking that there we might find safety for a while, Koreyoshi drove us out again, so that we could find no rest for our foot throughout all the length and breadth of the land.

"And so the next autumn arrived, and we who had always been wont to view the moon from the sacred enclosure of the Nine-fold Palace, now spent our nights watching it on the eight-fold sea-road. And in the tenth month, seeing that the Genji had driven us from the Capital, and we had been expelled from Kyushu by Koreyoshi, so that we were like a fish in a net having no place whither to escape, the Chūjō Kiyotsune, hating to live any longer, threw himself into the sea in despair. And this was but the beginning of our afflictions. Tossing on the waves by day, and spending our sleepless nights in the ships, we had no tribute of rice with which to prepare the Imperial Food, and sometimes, when we wished to prepare it, we had no water with which to do so. Afloat on the vast ocean we could not drink its salt water, and thus we underwent all the suffering of the Preta world. Then, after we had won two fights at Muroyama and Mizushima, the spirits of our family were revived, and building a fortress at Ichi-no-tani in the province of Settsu, all the Courtiers and Nobles doffed their court robes and clad themselves in armour for the fight, and the din of battle was incessant both by day and night, even like unto the battle of the Asuras with Indra and his Devas.

"Then in our flight after the defeat at Ichi-no-tani, parents were left behind by their children and wives separated from their husbands, and if we saw a fishing-boat in the offing we trembled lest it should be a ship of the enemy, while a flock of white herons in the pine-trees threw us into panic lest it should be the white flag of the Genji. And at last, when in the fight at Moji, Akama and Dan-no-ura she saw that our doom was sealed, the Nii-no-Ama weeping exclaimed: 'Now it seems our last hour has come, and in this fight there is little hope of any of the men surviving. Even if any of our distant relations are left alive they will scarcely be able to perform the services for our departed spirits, but from of old time it has been the custom to spare the women, so you must live to pray for the spirit of the Emperor, and I beg you also to say a prayer for my future salvation.'

"And as in a dream we listened to her words, of a sudden a great wind blew, and the drifting mist came down upon us, so that the hearts of the warriors were confounded, and in the face of heaven they could do nothing. Then the Nii-no-Ama took the Emperor into her arms and went to the gunwale of the vessel, and holding him tightly in her arms, leaped with him into the sea. My eyes darkened and my heart stood still, and it is a thing I can never forget or bear to think of. And at that moment from all those who still lived there went up so great and terrible a cry, that the shrieks of all the damned burning amid the hottest hell of Avichi could not exceed it.

"And so, after being roughly dragged out of the sea by the soldiers, as I was being sent back again to the Capital, I came to the shore of Akashi in the province of Harima. And as I chanced to fall asleep there for a space, I saw in a dream as it were our former Palace, but of greater and more surpassing beauty, and there sat our late Emperor with the Courtiers and Nobles of our house ranged about him in all their ceremonial grace and dignity; such a sight as I had not seen since we left our ancient Capital. And when I asked where this place might be, the Nii-no-Ama answered and said: 'This is called Ryūgū, the Palace of the Dragon King of the sea.'

"'Ah, how blessed!' I replied, 'and is it then a land where is no more sorrow?' 'In the Ryu-chiku Kyō you may read,' she said, 'and never neglect to pray fervently for our future happiness.' And as she said this I awoke, and since that time I have done nothing but read the Sutras and say the prayers for their future bliss, And all this, I think, is nothing else but the Six Paths." "In China," said the Hō-ō, "Hiuen

Tsiang saw the Six Paths before he received enlightenment, and in this country Nichizō Shōnin, by the
power of Zō-ō Gongen, is said to have seen them. That
you have been permitted to have gazed on them with
mortal eyes is a blessing indeed."

THE PASSING AWAY OF THE FORMER EMPRESS

But the boom of the bell of Jakkō-in proclaimed the
closing day as the evening sun began to sink in the
west, and His Majesty, full of regret at saying farewell, set out on his return journey with tears in his
eyes. The former Empress, her mind occupied in spite
of herself with thoughts of her bygone days, and
shedding on the sleeve of her robe the tears she could
not restrain, stood watching the Imperial Procession
until she could see it no more, and then, again entering
her cell, she prostrated herself before the Buddha to pray
that the Sacred Spirit of the former Emperor might
attain complete Buddhahood, and that the departed
spirits of all the Heike might quickly enter the Way of
Salvation.

In former days she turned to the east and prostrated
herself before the deity of the Great Shrine of Ise and
Sho-Hachimangu to pray; "That the Precious Life of
the Emperor may be prolonged a thousand and ten
thousand ages;" but now she sadly turned to the west
and prayed: "That the Departed Spirit may be reborn
in one of the Buddha Lands."

To express the regret and affection she still felt for

her past life, the Empress wrote these verses on the
shōji of her cell:

> In my present state
> Shall I ever hear again
> Tidings of my kin?
> Those who once attended me
> In the happy days at Court.

> Since those happy times—
> Like an unsubstantial dream—
> Now are past and gone;
> So may this rough brushwood hut
> Vanish, in its turn, away.

Moreover Tokudaiji Sadaisho Sanesada, one of the
Courtiers who accompanied the Hō-ō, also wrote these
lines on one of the posts of the cell:

> Once our Sovereign's face,
> Like the clear light of the moon,
> Shone on all around.
> Pent in this dark mountain vale,
> How can any moon be seen?

And while the former Empress was weeping and
meditating on the past and the future with pain mixed
with pleasure, the cry of the mountain cuckoo sounded
twice or thrice as the bird flew by, and suggested to
her these lines:

> So you measure, too,
> With my grief your mournful voice,
> Cuckoo of the vale.
> I, like you, have come to be
> Nothing but a plaintive cry.

Thus of the twenty survivors of the Heike who were
taken alive, some were paraded through the streets and
beheaded, and some were exiled to distant provinces,
far from their wives and children: with the excep-

The passing away of the Former Empress.

tion of Ike-no-Dainagon there was not one left living
in the Capital. Of the forty and more ladies who were
left nothing is known. They were taken in by their
kinsfolk and looked after by their relations. With
their hearts full of concealed regrets they spent their
days in lamentation.

Those in high places, up to the Emperor within the
Jewel Curtain, were filled with disquiet, while the common people, down to the dweller in the hut of brushwood, could find no rest. Husband and wife were
parted and far remote from the Palace, while parent
and child knew not each other's abode. And all this
was because of the many evil deeds of the Lay-priest
Chancellor Kiyomori which he continually committed,
in condemning people to death and banishing them, and
dismissing them from office and appropriating their
emoluments, without either regard for the Emperor on
his Throne, or pity for the people beneath him. So
certain is it that the good or evil deeds of the fathers
will descend upon the heads of the children.

But the former Empress continued to live on vainly
for some years, till at length she fell ill and took to her
bed. She had been awaiting her end for a long time,
and now she took in her hand the cord of five colours
that was fastened to the hand of the Buddha, and repeated the Nembutsu; "Namu Amida Nyorai, Lord
who guidest us to the Paradise of the West, in remembrance of thy Great Vow, I beseech thee receive me
into the Pure Land." And as she thus prayed, Dainagon-no-suke-no-Tsubone and Awa-no-Naiji, standing
on each side of her couch, lifted up their voices in

lamentation at their sad parting. And as the voice of her prayer grew weaker and weaker, a purple cloud of splendour grew visible in the west, and an unknown scent of wondrous incense filled the cell, while celestial strains of music were heard from above, and thus, about the middle of the second month of the second year of Ken-kyu, the former Empress Kenrei-mon-in breathed her last.

The two ladies, who had never left her side since the day that she had been chosen as Imperial Consort, were plunged into the depths of despair at this parting from their mistress, and as their relations and connections had all disappeared, and there was none to help them, they had nothing left but the performance of the Buddhist services. And at last they too, like the Dragon girl* who attained enlightenment, and like the lady Vaidehi,† also departed this life to be reborn in bliss.

---

*Or Naga maiden. Another example of a woman obtaining enlightenment, a thing that was regarded as difficult on account of the Five Hindrances, i.e. that woman cannot become either Brahma, Indra, Mara, a Tchakravartti, or a Buddha.

†The queen Vaidehi, wife of Bimbisara, king of Magadha, and mother of Ajatsattru who imprisoned her. At her earnest desire to hear the doctrine, Buddha miraculously flew to her prison and preached to her.

JAPAN	CONTEMPORARY EUROPE
	William of Malmesbury 1095-1142
	Song of Roland c.1100
	Geoffrey of Monmouth 1110-54
Taira Kiyomori born .. 1118	Knights Templar founded 1118
	Troubadours.
	Kalevala.
	Nibelungen Lied 1140
	Icelandic Sagas written 1140-1220
	Second Crusade 1147-49
	Frederick Barbarossa 1152-90
	Henry II of England 1154-89
Kiyomori becomes Chancellor of the Empire 1167	
Kiyomori becomes a Lay-priest 1168	Geoffroi de Villehardouin 1160-1213
The Ex-Emperor Go-Shira-kawa becomes Hō-ō or Cloistered Emperor .. 1169	Eleanor and Rosamund.
	Walther von der Vogelweide c.1160-1230
First plot of the Courtiers against Kiyomori .. 1177	Murder of Becket 1170
Retirement of the Emperor Takakura aet. 20, Accession of Antoku aet. 3.	
Revolt of Minamoto Yorimasa and Prince Takakura 1180	
Kiyomori removes the Capital to Fukuhara 1180	
Death of Kiyomori, aet. 63 1181	
Kiso Yoshinaka defeats the Heike in three battles 1182	
Heike flee the Capital, Yoshi-naka enters it 1183	

Death of Yoshinaka .. 1184	
Battle of Ichi-no-tani.	
Battle of Yashima, March 1185	
Battle of Dan-n o-u r a, April 1185	
Death of Yoshitsune .. 1189	Richard Coeur-de-Lion
Minamoto Yoritomo becomes Lord High Constable 1190	1189-99
Yoritomo becomes Shogun 1192	
Death of the Hō-ō Go-Shirakawa.	
Death of Yoritomo .. 1199	
	Wolfram von Eschenbach fl. c.1200

EMPERORS

Go-Shirakawa (1156-59)
    | (succ. aet 29, ret. 32, d. 65).

Nijo
Succ. aet (1159-65)
16, died
aet. 23,
    |
Rokujo
(1166-69)
Succ. 3, d. 13

(Mochihito
Prince Takakura)

Takakura
(1169-78)
Succ. 8, abdic.
20, d. 21
    |
Antoku   Go-Toba
(1181-83) (1184-98)

INDEX

INDEX

Other TUT BOOKS available:

Please order from your bookstore or write directly to:

CHARLES E. TUTTLE CO., INC.
Suido 1-chome, 2–6, Bunkyo-ku, Tokyo 112

or:

CHARLES E. TUTTLE CO., INC.
Rutland, Vermont 05701 U.S.A.